Introduction to the Pumpsaint Temple of the Stars

Jay Laville

In memory of my great, great grandmother, Ann Evans.

INDEX   <u>page</u>

4

Acknowledgements

This project would not have been undertaken were it not for the material published by Lewis Edwards and Katherine Maltwood. Being able to draw on the legacy of their work has been a fascinating experience and I have also greatly appreciated the work of the authors cited in 'References' at the end of this book.

I am sincerely grateful to Ordnance Survey. For copyright reasons, and for ease regarding scale, the illustrations in this book have been reproduced from the Ordnance Survey 'New Popular Edition One-Inch Map of England and Wales, Llandovery, Sheet 140', which was published in 1947.

I am indebted to Peter Sandover for the invaluable gift of dowsing rods; to Dewi for the generous donation of old, large-scale maps; to Kate Gooch for so kindly sharing her home on my visits to a similar 'Temple of the Stars' in the Glastonbury area; and to Pat Dermody for her greatly appreciated assistance and exchange of ideas. I am also thankful to the farmer and son at Troed-rhiw-ruddwen, near Rhandirmwyn, who rescued me and my car from a large heap of mud.

Finally, I am grateful to acquaintances, friends and family who have provided information, shown interest and given encouragement along the way.

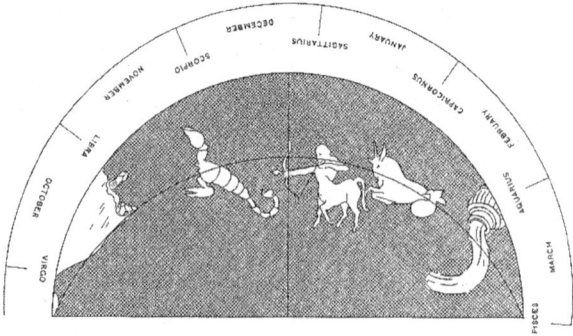

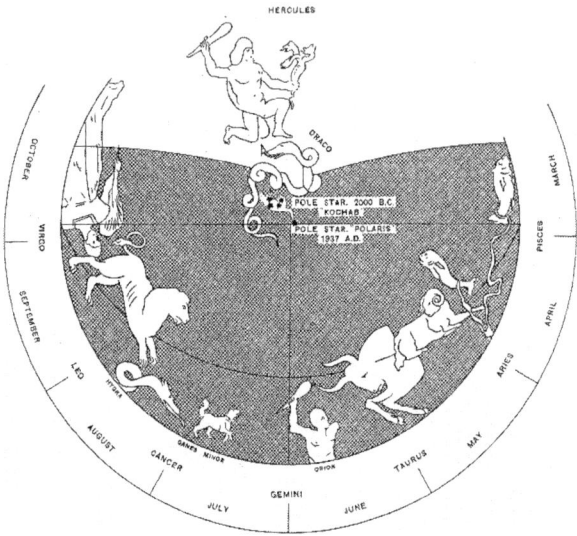

Maltwood's 'reproduced old drawing of the traditional constellation figures', (undated).

1
Introduction

In 1934, Katherine Maltwood published 'A Guide to Glastonbury's Temple of the Stars' which described how, etched into the landscape around Glastonbury, are correctly-placed outlines of symbols used to depict the signs of the zodiac (for example, fish for Pisces, a ram for Aries, a bull for Taurus, and so on).

Katherine Maltwood was a scholarly woman with an interest in Arthurian and Celtic myth and history. Drawing on the work of Edward Davies, she outlined the significance for ancient Britons of celebrating and marking the cycle of the year through their observations of the position of the stars. Indeed, it is widely recognised that they understood and predicted accurately the movement of the stars, with many of their monuments positioned to align with celestial events.

The Glastonbury Temple of the Stars is a replication, on the earth, of the annual movement of the constellations in the night sky. It is important to understand the sacred meaning that these sites would have held for the early Celts.

Edward Davies was a Christian minister residing in the county of Glamorgan. His book, 'The Mythology and Rites of the British Druids', 1809, was a sincere attempt to understand the British Druid tradition based on Roman written accounts, early Welsh manuscripts, mythology and Celtic artefacts, all of which he aimed to translate and interpret with academic rigour.

Versions of the story of Noah and his ark are found across many cultures and religions. In the legend, Noah and his wife, along with breeding pairs of every species of animal, boarded an ark so that they could survive relentless rain and flood waters which were to cause all other life forms upon the earth to be extinguished.

Davies purported that, similarly, the early Welsh Druid tradition was 'arkite' and of Hebrew origin, with Phoenician influence. In his book he demonstrated that the sun, moon and stars represented multiple deities for the Druids; the natural world was sacred and worship was conducted in sanctuaries, or temples, outdoors.

Central to the Druid arkite mysteries were 'Hu' and 'Ceridwen'. Davies describes 'Hu' as a Noah figure who was revered as the sun god; the Welsh word for 'sun' is 'Huan'. While 'Lugh' is the better-known Celtic sun god and may be synonymous with 'Hu'; for the sake of consistency with Davies' translations, the term 'Hu' will be used throughout this book. In the oral bardic tradition, Hu was often symbolised as a bull, ox, a lion or an eagle.

Ceridwen was the equivalent of Noah's wife and was the divine force guiding the ark safely through the deluge; she was represented by many symbols including a cauldron, a greyhound bitch, a hawk, an otter, an egg, a hen and the containing ark itself. In some myths she is associated with the moon.

Importantly, Davies observed that ancient Britons used the same phrase 'Caer Sidi' to refer to the zodiac and, also, to their sacred temples. Today, the Welsh word for zodiac is

'Sidydd'. Davies proposed that the celestial temples referred to by the Welsh bards were likely to contain not just the constellations of the zodiac representations, but also of the sun god and Ceridwen, who they worshipped.

Davies concluded that it would be of value to discover these sanctuaries "in which our ancestors celebrated the rites of their Ceridwen or Ceres, and performed other acts of worship". Katherine Maltwood's discovery of the Glastonbury representations of the zodiac was a significant breakthrough in this regard.

In 1947 and 1948, Lewis Edwards, published a series of articles in *Atlantean Research* suggesting that the landscape around Pumpsaint, in Carmarthenshire, had also been shaped to depict the symbols of the constellations of the night-sky. He titled this work 'The Welsh Temple of the Zodiac'.

To the ancient Celts, gold was a representation of the sun, so it is not insignificant that Pumpsaint is home to a rich source of gold-carrying quartz and the Dolaucothi gold mines. This hallowed sanctuary contained, at its heart, the sun god himself.

There is evidence of bronze-age working at the Dolaucothi site; later it was extensively mined by the Romans until the 5th century AD and then lay dormant until the 19th century. Gold finally ceased to be mined there in 1938.

Nowadays, we are familiar with the depiction of the celestial constellations in the form of a printed zodiac, with its twelve signs. However, over the ages, the symbols used to portray the constellations have varied, both in their image and in number.

The constellation sites initially proposed by Lewis Edwards involved outlines covering a substantial acreage, often over rugged, precipitous land and unable to be seen as a whole from the ground. Their construction would have depended on sophisticated astronomical and mathematical awareness and considerable labour.

In researching Edwards' claims, Ian Henning in 'The Pumpsaint Zodiac: Reality Lost and Fantasy Found', points out that it is now accepted that the ancient Nazca outlines in the Peruvian desert, for example, were designed so as to be seen as a whole only from above. Moreover, Edwards' ideas were not likely to be merely fanciful; he was an intelligent and religious man who had held responsible positions under Ramsay McDonald and Lord Portal.

In 'The Ancient Paths', 2013, Graham Robb brings to the fore the extraordinary depth and breadth of learning undertaken by the Druids, who's rigorous training lasted around 20 years, involved study of the sciences and arts and would have included subjects such as mathematics, engineering, law, philosophy, geometry, mythology and astronomy.

The Celtic architects, therefore, would have applied extensive knowledge to the planning and construction of the Pumpsaint sanctuary, which was designed to incorporate the central symbols of their beliefs. The result is a precise and impressive work of sacred geography, sitting within at least a 12-mile radius of the Dolaucothi gold mines (page 16).

It is suggested that the Glastonbury and Pumpsaint zodiac symbols would have been crafted as offerings to the heavens, as well as bringing to earth representations from the sky. Entering into one of these earth-sculpted temples would be to enter into a relationship with both the sanctified earth and the gods they represented.

My involvement with the Pumpsaint Zodiac happened without much forethought. After my grandmother's death in 1998, many of her esoteric books were gifted to me by my Uncle. They included Katherine Maltwood's 'Air View Supplement to A Guide to Glastonbury's Temple of the Stars', 1937.

At mid-winter in 2001, I received an unexpected present of dowsing rods, fashioned from paint-bucket handles. They have proved very useful, helping me to locate electrical wires beneath plaster, water pipes, old tracks or leys, mislaid objects and, on one occasion, when lost in the Cambrian Mountains, a direct route back to my car several miles away. I don't have an explanation for how they work.

In 2009, in quick succession, three people separately mentioned that there was supposed to be a Welsh land-zodiac. I was interested to know more and, after hearing about it for the third time and that it was meant to be in the Pumpsaint area, I decided to undertake field-work, dowsing for the outlines. A few days later, on Saturday 8th August 2009, I set off from my home in mid-Wales to begin searching for the temple sites.

A prior internet search revealed that some investigations had already been undertaken by the Morien Institute and their article gave good information about the work of Lewis Edwards and where the individual outlines of each zodiac symbol might be found. I decided to begin with Aquarius and make progress from there. Over the ensuing years, I simply held a dowsing rod with intent, followed the direction it pointed to and mapped the routes taken.

As predicted by Edward Davies in 1809, the shapes which emerged on the maps correspond not just to the signs of the zodiac, but also to representations of the sun god, Hu, and Ceridwen. All are 'upright' when viewed on a map and from the south. Most are clearly defined images but, as can be seen from the missing tail of the 'horse' of Sagittarius, I have not been able to complete every feature.

Some symbols are partially overlapping; therefore, one outline needed to be given priority over another on the coloured map of the front cover. For example, the depiction of Taurus is particularly compromised, but fuller features can be found at the start of chapter 7. Additionally, symbols within the outer boundaries of the sanctuary have been identified and are subject to ongoing investigation.

As mentioned earlier, the illustrations in this book have been reproduced from the Ordnance Survey 'New Popular Edition One-Inch Map of England and Wales, Llandovery, Sheet 140', which was published in 1947. The main advantage of doing so is that, where removal and alterations of paths and roads have taken place in recent times, the original routes maybe shown. However, footpaths are, generally, not so clearly marked and pertinent ancient tracks, which I have walked and which are shown on more recent maps, are sometimes not shown at all. An example of this is a significant track across Mynydd Mallaen which has two standing stones, as well as large stones of white quartz, marking the route. The 1947 map shows just one of the standing stones and no track at all.

The illustrations produced in this book are not completely accurate; a few footpaths, which are either missing on the 1947 map or obscured by other detail, are hand-drawn. Inaccuracies also result from small movements of the tracing paper used when reproducing outlines. Minor changes in the spelling of place names may be noticed as they have altered over time.

Ordnance Survey Explorer maps, numbers 186, 187 and 199, were helpful companions when walking the areas covered by this project. To check the consistency of routes over time, I also referred to the 'One-Inch Map of Great Britain, Llandovery, Sheet 140, 1967'.

The outlines of each zodiac sign are mainly formed by embanked, purposely-constructed by-ways which have the approximate width of a single-track, country lane. Some of these routes have become tarmac roads; otherwise, they are nearly always recognised rights of way. Very occasionally, part of an outline is delineated by the course of a river, or a boundary wall, instead.

Graham Robb draws attention to the fact that the early European Celts migrated often and Druids, therefore, came from many origins and would have had "many realms of folklore". It follows, then, that what is presented here is very much a Welsh Druidic story, captured in the rhymes and riddles of the Welsh bards, and immortalised through its inscription, in this instance, on the soil of Carmarthenshire and Ceredigion. It is thought that there are other celestial temples in Wales.

While it is likely that Druidic sanctuaries across Britain will share similar features, there will be local differences, too, to reflect legends particularly relevant to where they are sited.

To begin with, cross-country rights of way were dowsed on foot. This was by far the best way to discover remnants of an ancient past, such as the unmapped standing stones keeping a lonely vigil of the wild, sacred places that they mark. Stretches of road were dowsed at various points to confirm the route. If a response couldn't be found at a place where an outline was supposed to be, I would map-dowse to find a different starting position.

In the recent few years, I have developed a physical condition which makes walking long distances unfeasible, so I have combined map-dowsing with dowsing just part of a footpath, starting from a roadside position where a potentially relevant track begins or finishes.

It is my intention that this first book about the 'Pumpsaint Temple' introduces the basic outlines and geographical locations of the individual constellation-symbols, but not of all the details found within each representation. For example, later in the book is described the outline of an eagle, but not the additional relevant paths which define its feather-layers.

My hope is that people will come to this beautiful part of Wales and personally discover the more intricate imagery of the zodiac-signs and gain their own insights into the symbolic meanings they hold.

The key to the secrets of these sites belongs to a long-past oral tradition; however, some references are preserved in old records of the early Celts and, more generally, in mythology and archaeology. As a result, there are many theories and threads of interest to follow; more work is needed in order to consider them at greater depth.

Overall, the search for the 'Pumpsaint Temple of the Stars' has drawn me into a stunningly beautiful, mysterious and potent landscape which holds within its form, wild, ancestral and atmospheric locations.   I have found that the constellation symbols are etched onto the earth with artistry, proportion and detail and that the zodiac sites are often scattered with standing stones, burial mounds, cairns, stone circles and hill forts.

Very occasionally, dowsing has indicated a route which must have been a right of way in the past, but is no longer accessible – please don't trespass. Given the passage of time, it is remarkable that the outlines of the sites are still, to this day, largely made up of identifiable footpaths, tracks, and even pertinent footbridges and that so much of this early temple-landscape remains our privilege to experience.

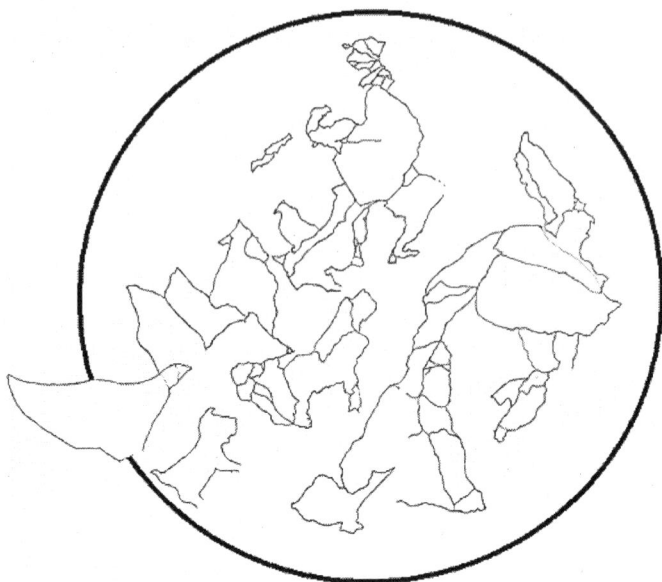

Constellation Outlines of the Pumpsaint Temple of the Stars, 2017

2

The 'arkite' mysteries in Celtic Wales

In 'The Mythology and Rites of the British Druids', Edward
Davies described that the early bards told of a ceremonial
rite, a "solemn procession" whereby Hu's symbolic chariot,
or shrine, was drawn out of the waters by sacred bulls and
pulled from one place to another; a ritual which was similarly
described in Phoenician and German mythology.

In the Welsh arkite legend, the beaver (in Welsh *'Avanc'*), is
pulled out of the waters by the sacred oxen of Hu (*'Ychen
Banaug'*). It is unlikely that an actual beaver was drawn out
of the floods, given that early documents reveal that it was
such a strenuous task that one of the three bulls involved
collapsed and died.

Davies proposed that the word 'beaver' *(Avanc)* was perhaps
used to describe the ark which, itself, held representations of
both a masculine deity and a feminine one, to the early Celts.
It was the male, Noah, who was the builder of the ark and
Davies told that, correspondingly, a beaver is "a most
distinguished architect. He is said to build a house of two
stories; one of which is in the water, and the other above the
water; and out of the latter, he has an egress to dry ground".

However, Davies also translated that it was the female,
Noah's wife, Ceridwen, who was the "genius of the ark"; the
intelligent presence who guided the vessel through the flood.
The ark symbolises, then, the necessary union of masculine
and feminine principles in order to bring the fullness of life to
fruition.

As late as 1809, Edward Davies recalled that "Of all the objects of ancient superstition, there is none which has taken hold of the populace of Wales, as the celebrated *oxen of Hu*. Their fame is still vigorous in every corner of the principality, as far, at least, as the Welsh language has maintained its ground".

At the same time, he acknowledged that the origins and meaning of the legend were largely lost; "Few indeed, pretend to tell us precisely, what the *Ychen Banaug* were, or what the *Avanc* was, which they drew out of the lake". To the Druids, this rite ensured that the land would not be flooded again.

The very persistence of the legend demonstrates not only the enormous importance of this early rite, but also that neither the Roman occupation, nor the spread of Christianity, were able to extinguish the influence of early Celtic spirituality from all parts of Wales.

Indeed, Davies reported that Hywel ab Owain Gwynedd, the bardic Prince of Gwynedd, who died in the 12th century, was initiated into the lesser and greater Druidic mysteries; and credible evidence that authentic Druid practice continued into the middle of the 14th century is preserved in the written accounts of Madawg Dwygbaig, penned between the years 1290 to 1340. Furthermore, Davies told that "Dyfed was so entirely devoted to the mysteries of druidism, that it was said to have been anciently enveloped in *Llengel, a concealing veil*; and it was by way of eminence, denominated *Gwldd Yr Hud*, the *land of mystery*".

Drawing on what is assumed to be the bardic prose of Gwyddnaw, Davies described a final rite of Druidic initiation: "Here the noviciate was committed to the sea, which represented the *deluge*, in a *close coracle,* the symbol of the *ark;* and after the example of the *just patriarch*, was to be saved from this image of the flood, at Gwyddnaw's *wear* (weir), the type of *mount* of debarkation". Not all candidates would complete, or even survive, the test; but if achieved, the secrets of the greater Druid mysteries would be revealed to them.

The experience of being pulled from the waters was endured, too, by the great bard, Taliesin, who told that he was born three times; once of his natural parents as 'Gwion the Little'; once of shape-shifting Ceridwen, after he was ingested by her when she was in the form of a hen and he as a seed of corn; and lastly, he was born of a mystical coracle as it was pulled out of the waters at a weir by Elphin, who named him 'Taliesin' meaning 'radiant brow'.

In keeping with the Druidic oral tradition, there are many hidden meanings to be found within the symbolism of these accounts. What is certain, though, is that being 'born' of the sacred vessel was a most holy rite of passage.

3

Ceridwen

Caer-Cadwgan

Tan-las

Bryn Mawr

Garreg
Hirfaen

Blaen
Hathren

Symbol: A hen

In legend, Ceridwen has several representations including
that of a "black, high-crested hen", as told in Davies'
translation of Hanes Taliesin.   Before describing the outlines
of the zodiac constellations within the temple, the nature of
Ceridwen and her distinctive outline within the temple-
boundary, warrant attention.

While the Druid tradition was rooted in a patriarchal era,
Ceridwen had a central role in the Druidic arkite mysteries.
The respect given to Ceridwen, as well as the celebration,
rather than suppression, of her mystical and regenerative
powers, was perhaps indicative of the fact that the position
of Celtic women was one of relative strength for those times.

Celtic law, for example, was more favourably disposed to the marriage and inheritance rights of women than Roman law.

In his book, 'The Mythology and Rites of the British Druids', Davies explained that 'cauldron' was a term associated with Ceridwen and that she was well-read in astronomy, botany and the properties of herbs. In the Druid training, the 'cauldron' was "used metaphorically to imply the whole mass of doctrine and discipline, together with the confined circle, of arts and sciences, which pertained to the ancient priesthood of Britain." He goes on to describe that the most sacred of the Druid mysteries were unable to be celebrated by an initiate until the cauldron had been properly prepared.

Moreover, Davies tells, it was Ceridwen who presided over the "cauldron of Awen", the "water of inspiration, sciences and immortality" and that this containing vessel represented something of the mysteries themselves. Immortality being a matter of the soul, Ceridwen had a potent and priestly role.

The hen's outline can be found on the south-east outskirts of Lampeter, on the other side of Afon Teifi. Several features suggestive of an ancient past can be seen on this quiet farmland; including partially-collapsed mounds and stones of possible significance.

❖ From Lan-las, a footpath heading north-east is taken. It joins a short stretch of lane and comes to a fork. Bearing right and continuing in a north-easterly direction, quickly leads to a fork in the path. Here, if the left fork is taken, a crossroad of tracks is soon reached, from which, if a right-turn in a southeastwardly direction to Ty'n-y-coed, the hen's crest is formed.

- ❖ At the fork, however, the main route leads east, south-eastwards, until the track joins a lane continuing south-eastwards. When these directions from Lan-las are followed, the top of the hen's beak and its head and back are delineated.

- ❖ From Lan-las, taking an eastwards direction, then curving southwards, the lane turns into a green road, past Bryn-Mawr, until it reaches Blaen-Hathren. This depicts the outline of the lower beak and the hen's front and feet.

- ❖ To complete the outline of the hen, just to the east of Blaen-Hathren is a boundary wall running north-eastwards, past Carreg-hirfaen; however, there is no right of way to walk this final part of the route.

Carreg-hirfaen is a tall standing stone with unusual diagonal markings. In 1947, Lewis Edwards wrote, "In a field close to Hirfaen there existed a wattle and daub church. A stone paving led from the standing stone Hirfaen to the church. The paving was only removed a generation ago and its removal is recorded". This extraordinary description symbolises that, to inhabitants of the area, the old and new religions were mutually inclusive; both could inform their worship; a path could be found between the two.

4

Aquarius

Symbol – A beaver.

Aquarius is an air sign but its depiction in today's zodiac is 'the water-bearer', originating from images of the Egyptian water-god, Hapi, who watered the earth from two jugs. Aquarius can be seen as symbolising the watery aspect of air.

This effigy was described by Lewis Edwards as a squirrel. However, Ian Henning proposed that it is a beaver, explaining that these creatures were still in existence on the nearby Afon Teifi in the 12th century, according to Gerald of Wales in 1188. Given the importance of the beaver in the arkite mythology of the early Welsh Druids, along with the beaver's natural affinity with both air and water and the outline's distinctly beaver-like appearance, it is described here as a beaver.

The outline of Aquarius can be found a few miles from Lampeter, on the B4343, in the area of Llanfair Clydogau. It takes in the summit of Bryn Cysegrfa, which translates evocatively as 'Hill of the Sacred Place'. Along the fence-line between the rowan-lined, mountain road and Bryn Cysegrfa, there are occasional small standing stones, or marker stones. Once, Bryn Cysegrfa would have been open land, but now it is fenced into fields. Despite this, it has an uplifting sense of freedom, of unboundaried space and of hallowed ground.

A standing stone is reported to have once stood on Bryn Cysegrfa and Ian Henning states it is possible that it now occupies Llanddewi-Brefi church and is known as St David's staff. Henning recalls hearing a story that St David, of the 6th century, "slew the beaver" with the standing stone. This legend is also referred to in 'The Ancient Stones of Wales' by Barber and Williams and, in keeping with early Christian church edict, may describe a deliberate dismantling of the sacred temple-site and a triumphant exhibition of having done so; symbolically, it would have been a forceful establishment of the new religion over the old. To the Druids, it would have been a deeply wounding event.

In several fields beyond Bryn Cysegrfa, towards Llanddewi-Brefi, there are a few heaps of very large stones. There is no firm evidence that they are significant, but they seem out of keeping with the surrounding mountain meadow-land and evoke thoughts about where they came from and whether they were once part of the ancient sanctuary.

  ❖ At the time of visiting the site of Aquarius, some of the local footpath signs had been removed; however, to define the outline of the beaver, starting from

Llanfair Clydogau and taking a peaceful old track east, south-eastwards running beside Nant Clywedog, the underbelly of the beaver is formed.

❖ As this route joins a lane and curves around to Troed-y-bryn and approximately northwards to Pont Glanrhyd, it shapes the foreleg of the beaver.

❖ The neck and head of the beaver are created by leaving Pont Glanrhyd in a north-westwards direction and quickly picking up a footpath on the right which traverses the lower slopes of Bryn Cysegrfa, towards Pengelli'r Bryn; here, the way bears left, westwards, running along a track past Glan-crwys, Gwar-fford and Plas-yr-allt, to the B4343.

❖ At the B4343, a left-turn is taken briefly, before a turn on the right is taken to Waun-wen and Afon Teifi, to complete the outline of the beaver's back.

❖ A small track running beneath the pillow mounds on Bryn Cysegrfa delineates the beaver's head from its body.

❖ The bushy tail of the beaver can be reached by heading from the church at Llanfair Clydogau to cross the river at Pont Llanfair. The outline can be followed by bearing right at the Post Office and right again at the slightly altered entrance to Parcneuadd, where evidence of the significant original path remains.

- ❖ At Parcneuadd itself, one side of the tail-outline follows the river up to just above Penddol, but there is no right of way. The other side is defined by a footpath up to Clwt-y-patrwm, Pencaerodyn and Blaencyswch. At Blaencyswch, a right-turn is taken and the lane followed to a boundary-line running back to Penddol; again there is no defined footpath on this final part of the route.

On the path from Parcneuadd to Clwt-y-patrwm, I spoke with a farmer and asked him what he knew about Bryn Cysegrfa. Indicating to it across the valley, he recounted that he had grown up with a story that a long, long time ago local people had wanted to build a church there and, searching for the right words, he described it as "consecrated land". Place names often hold descriptions and meanings which have been lost in the aeons of time. Befitting of its name, though, Bryn Cysegrfa continues to be held in local memory as a sacred place.

5

Pisces

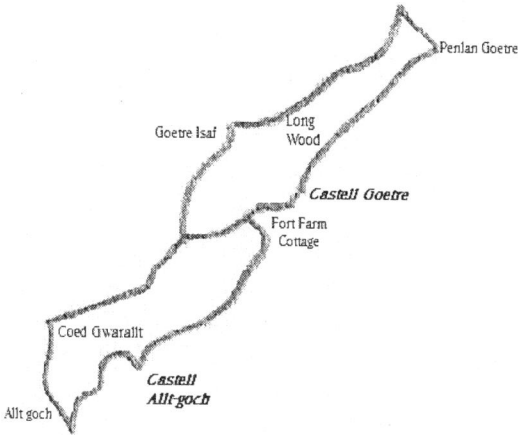

Symbol – Two fish.

With the female species of a fish having a more developed dorsal fin, depicted here is a male and a female fish, the female being on the left.

Pisces is positioned on a ridge which rises up from the north-east of the town of Lampeter. To the west and south-west of the ridge are the remains of two castles – Castell Olwen and Castell Bugad. On the ridge itself, are placed two further iron-age forts, named Castell Allt-goch and Castell Goetre, described by Ceredigion local government to have been constructed around the 2nd or 3rd century BC.

Lewis Edwards believed the main entrance to the zodiac temple to be placed here; certainly, many paths lead up to the site from different directions, indicating that this would have been a place of some significance; however, other possible gateways to the sanctuary will be described later.

Approaching the Piscean site from the direction of Lampeter Rugby Club and bearing left at Mount Pleasant Farm along a stony-bottomed track lined with mature beech trees, it is evident that this is an old and purposeful track.

Beech is not native to central Wales, so these stately trees were planted with intention and perhaps to make a statement about the importance of the route. In fact, much of the way along the outline of Pisces is beech-lined, as are some sections along the boundaries of the other zodiac signs.

Thomas Pakenham, in his book, 'Meetings with Remarkable Trees', tells that beech trees tend not to live for more than 200 years which suggests that, until relatively recent times, the outlines of the individual sites making up the Pumpsaint Temple of Stars were being marked and, perhaps, still recognised as having spiritual and ancestral significance.

In many parts of Britain, expressions of Celtic spirituality persisted for centuries, co-existing and inter-mingling with Christian practice without too much difficulty. Old churches were often built on pre-Christian holy sites and, sometimes, with symbols of early nature-religion sculpted into the very fabric of their structures; such as 'green man' images which were once carved into numerous church roof bosses and corbels.

Neglect and destruction of the temple sites have taken their toll across the ages. In 'The Mythology and Rites of the British Druids', Davies revealed how, in the 6th century AD, the sites were deliberately desecrated, quoting the lament of the bards "they land in the celestial circle . . . over the pale white boundary. The grey stones they actually remove".

More recently, in 1947, there was a stone circle shown to be placed between the two Piscean hill-forts; it is now missing and, by 1967, it was no longer mapped. Generally across the temple sites, many standing stones have disappeared. Some have been taken as trophies; others have been re-used for utilitarian purposes, such as for the construction of footbridges across streams, or as gateposts. Barber and Williams describe that many standing stones across Wales have been destroyed.

- ❖ The outline of Pisces was found by starting on the south-western reaches of Coed-Gwarallt and continuing along an unmapped track which runs along the southern edge of the woodland, north-eastwards to Castell Allt-goch; this forms the bottom of the tail of the fish on the left.

- ❖ Reaching Castell Allt-goch, the dowsing rod unexpectedly swung away from the track to follow the outside curve of the fort embankment until a large stone of white, glinting quartz was reached. Here, the rod swung back to re-join the well-trodden footpath a bit further along and this whole process created an outline of a small fin.

Along the route, are standing stones at two gateways, with white quartz placed at their base. A couple of smaller stones in the vicinity are marked with a neatly engraved symbol, not dissimilar to the three rays of the Druidic 'awen' sign, under a horizontal line:

$$\overline{/|\backslash}$$

The same sign can be seen on stones at other ancient sites, such as on a cist stone above Coed Dyffryn, near Neath, and on a stone at the base of Glastonbury Tor. The precise and uniform symbols have a relatively modern appearance and give rise to questions about how they were carved, when and why.

- ❖ The underneath of the two fishes' heads are formed by continuing along a track from Castell Allt-goch, curving eastwards to Fort Farm Cottage and then on to the tranquil site of Castell Goetre, with its lumps of white quartz on the bank of the fort, alongside the footpath.

- ❖ After Castell Goetre, the next part of the way runs alongside Long Wood to Penlan Goetre and then returns along a parallel track running back through the woodland itself.

- ❖ Towards the western end of Long Wood, a dowser may be confusingly directed towards Betws Bledrws away from the effigy of Pisces altogether. After a few yards in this direction, however, a left-turn along an overgrown old track, on the very edge of the wood, is indicated. This soggy route quickly rejoins

the newer path back to Lampeter, curving
southwards on its western edge to re-join the
starting place at Coed Gwarallt.

Before leaving the woods, it is possible to take a small detour
to the signposted and intriguing 'Hobb's garden', which lies
within the boundaries of the outline. Along this path, art and
the outdoors converge; offerings surround a mysterious,
otherworldly being; and a theatre of nature unfolds beneath
a whispering green canopy, amidst shards of dancing light.
Don't be surprised if you depart this sanctuary with a sense
that the old Druids haven't quite gone away.

6

Aries

Cwmann

A485

site of old Ram Inn

Ram

Ddeunant

Rhiwlas

A482

Brynmanalog

Settlement

Settlement

Blaenycwm

Hendre-las

Mynydd Pencarreg

Pant-y-fan

Esgair-Dawe Farm

Cae-Mawr

Symbol – A ram

The site of Aries lies just outside Lampeter to the South-West and, satisfyingly, it is situated in the parish of Ram. At the start of this project, there was a 'Ram Inn' pub sign, but the property has since been turned into a private dwelling and the sign removed.

The detail in the outline of Aries demonstrates the care that these effigies were given in their construction. In the image above, the eye positioned near the site of an old quarry is included for visual effect to show the corresponding eyelid shape on the ram's head.

* The face of the ram is defined by taking a south-eastwards direction from the site of the old Ram Inn, along the lane, past Tal-y-fedw, to Rhiwlas.

* At Rhiwlas, there is no footpath leading to the A482, to create the ram's nose. However, the dowsing rod persistently pointed along the line of a field-boundary just past Rhiwlas, towards the main road. Standing at vantage points to better view the 'out-of-bounds' route, it was possible to see that there are several very large stones, lying prone, at the edge of the fields.

* Checking this part of the outline from the A482, itself, just south of Gelli-wrol, the rod swung towards Rhiwlas, indicating a well-worn piece of ground along a field boundary, to form the ram's jaw.

* The outline of the face of the ram is completed by following the A482 from Gelli-wrol back to the parish of Ram and the site of the old Ram Inn.

Lewis Edwards described that he was uncertain as to which way the ram should be facing, but that, on an old 16th century map with a different road layout, it appears to be facing backwards and looking towards the west; in the same way as the ram in the Glastonbury zodiac. However, on an antiquated Indian zodiac the ram of Aries was shown to be looking forwards, towards the east. Unfortunately, the date and source of the old Indian document referred to by Edwards are not known, so cannot be compared. My own findings are that the head of the ram in the Pumpsaint zodiac was found to be looking forward, in an eastwards direction.

❖ The top of the Ram's head is defined by following the
A482 from the site of the old Ram Inn, north-
westwards towards Lampeter; then, south-
westwards along the A485 to the first turning on the
left.

❖ Turning off the A485, to Ddeunant, the lane forms
part of the Ram's horn. From Ddeunant, a right-turn
is taken; here an unmapped standing stone is tucked
into the hedgerow and the horn is beautifully shaped
as it bends and curves westwards to re-join the A485.

❖ On reaching the A485, it is evident that the road back
towards Lampeter has been straightened. On the
northern side of the A485, the curved piece of old
road is still in existence and is the significant route.

After leaving Ddeunant, before following the rest of the
route, it is possible to turn left at Brynmanalog to visit the
ancient hill-settlements which lie within the effigy of Aries.
Graham Robb describes that such sites were not always
defensive constructions but were often used for
administrative and sacred purposes and, at times, may have
been developed on pre-existing, more ancient sites.

❖ At Ddeunant, the ram's outline follows a country lane
to Brynmanalog, Fro-wen and Pant-y-fen, where it
takes a left-turn across the open mountain land of
Mynydd Pencarreg until it bears left at a crossroad of
possible paths.

❖ Before reaching Pantyfyd Uchaf, the outline of Aries
turns away from this track along a footpath on the

left, past Cae-Mawr and continuing in a northwards direction to Esgair-Dawe Farm; here, the route follows the lane in a northwards direction to Blaenycwm.

❖ At Blaenycwm, a footpath on the left is taken which runs past Pant-y-rhedyn to a T-junction of tracks, where the right hand path is taken, to join the A482 at Ty-Hywel. At Ty-Hywel, a left-turn is taken along the A482, to Tygwilym, completing the outline of the ram's body.

The quartz-containing track leading across Mynydd Pencarreg has an open, timeless feel and the route is lined, in part, with wind-bent old hawthorn and rowan trees planted on raised banks.

I was to find the presence of quartz on many of the outline-paths. Could it be that the pieces of white quartz, now embedded into soil and vegetation, were scattered on the surface of the ancient routes when the temple was first constructed? Davies' translation of the bard's proclamation that "they land in the celestial circle . . . over the pale white boundary" is suggestive of a visibly clear demarcation.

Barber and Williams reported the widespread presence of quartz stone in the ancient sites of Wales and found that the stones generate radio-signal interference. In more recent times, the properties of quartz have been utilised in watches, radio receivers and for programming.

Ancient knowledge about the qualities of quartz may have continued to exert an influence in sacred construction far beyond the times that these aged stone monuments were erected. At Cilycwm, for example, white quartz has been incorporated into the church building and, at Caio and at Pant-Yr-Eglwys, seams of white-quartz capstones top the churchyard walls.

Freddy Silva attributes the use of quartz in ancient temples to its ability to produce a change in the energy-field and to bring about altered awareness. In Davies' translation, the Welsh bard, Aneurin, in the 6th century AD, described the "blessed sanctuary" as "the chief place of distribution of the source of energy".

The Druid priests of the Pumpsaint temple would have understood the energetic properties of their quartz-containing stones and would have presided over their ceremonial purpose in these places of power.

7

Taurus

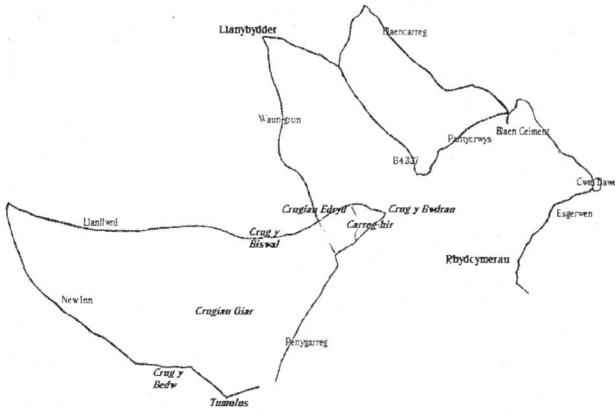

Symbol – A winged bull and ark

Edward Davies described that throughout the ages, in religions across the world, the bull and ox have been used interchangeably to represent the mythological embodiment of the source of energy, the god of the sun. Early examples of bull worship have been discovered in an old sacred sanctuary of eastern Anatolia, in the form of preserved bulls' heads; they date from the Neolithic period, around the 8th century BC.

The 'winged bull', as in this terrestrial zodiac, has a very ancient history, perhaps originating from the Lamassu statue which was believed to date from the 13th century BC. The Lamassu statue was a winged bull with human head which stood in Nimrud, in Iraq, until it was destroyed during civil unrest, in 2015. It is thought that the city of Nimrud was named after Nimrod, the great-grandson of Noah.

The presence of the outline of a winged bull in the Pumpsaint zodiac-temple offers support for Davies' proposal that the Druid arkite mysteries are of eastern origin.

- ❖ To form the outline of the bull's head; just above Caermalwas Fawr (on the B4337 from Rhydcymerau to Llanybydder), a right-turn towards Pantycrwys is taken and followed in an east, north-easterly direction. Near Pantycrwys, in a field on the right, is a nicely shaped standing stone; perhaps the bardic "sacred rock" in the "hall of the Ox", as translated by Davies.

- ❖ Further along, the track meets three others and, there, the rod indicated two pertinent routes, the first being southwards towards Blaen Ceiment, to give shape to the bull's ear.

- ❖ However, the main outline of the head of Taurus continues north-eastwards briefly and then turns south-eastwards, past Pantyfyd Uchaf and Galltyfydr towards Cwm Dawe.

This site for Taurus is not the same as that suggested by Lewis Edwards and I began to doubt my findings, concerned that there had been no indication of a bull's horn. Also, near Cwm Dawe, the dowsing rod insisted that the original route crossed a small field (now hedged and not a right of way), to form a perfect bull's nose-ring. I felt sure a nose-ring must be a fairly modern invention.

However, later research revealed that, from the earliest recorded times, nose-rings were used on cattle and horses in ancient Sumer, as can be seen on the 'Standard of Ur' which originates from around 2,500 BC. Moreover, horns were removed for the ease of handling.

* From Cwm Dawe, the route bears westwards towards Maestyle. Before reaching Maestyle, a path on the left is followed, to Esgerwen. After Esgerwen a partially unmapped track on the left continues southwards, past Cwmcoedifor to the B4337; completing the outline of the bull's head.

* One of the bull's wings is delineated by returning to the crossroad of paths above Blaen-Ceiment and following the route north-westwards, all the way to Blaencarreg. At Blaencarreg, a left-turn onto a footpath running south-westwards is taken, until a right-turn is needed, to briefly follow the lane past Llwynmadyn, before the route takes a left turn onto an old green road past Pen-lan and arrives at the B4337, completing the wing-outline.

* The second wing is defined by following the B4337 from near Bwlch Caermalwas, in a north, north-westerly direction to the crossroad at Llanybydder. Here, a left-turn is taken onto the A485 for a short while, before another left-turn onto a lane, bearing southwards. This route skirts past the distinctive hill-fort of Pen y gaer and peters out to become a very old track. The way continues to a crossroad of paths, where it bears left and runs past Crugiau Edryd, to a tarmac road.

The terrain to the west of the bull is very sacred indeed. Set amidst an area laden with mystery and age is a large expanse of open skies and grassy mountain-land. Here can be found many circular mounds which were probably funereal in nature: Crugiau Giar, Crug Bedw, Crugiau Edryd, Crug y Bwdran, and Crug y Biswal. These were no ordinary cairns, but prominent burial mounds; those interned here would have had significant status and would have been honoured by the Druids with respectful and reverent ceremony.

Allcroft, in 'Circle and The Cross', described the ancient tradition of burying the dead within a circle and Koch explains that, to the early Celts, the west was the place of the ancestors and of the 'otherworld', which could be accessed through portals such as burial mounds.

Connected, but in forestry planted since 1947, to the south are Crugiau Rhos-wen and Crugyn Amlwg. They sit on Mynydd Tre-beddau, mountain of the graves; further south, again, are several more significant ritual and funerary sites.

This landscape was mentioned by Edward Lewis, who noted the alignment of the tumuli in position to one another, and posed that Crug y Biswal pointed to the era in which the temple was constructed, which he felt to be around 4,500BC. This is now recognised to be unlikely; in his article 'The Origin of the Zodiac', Gary Thompson explains that the Babylonian zodiac was the origin of all zodiacs and began to be gradually developed from around 1,300 BC.

Thompson states that today's zodiac would have developed in stages; the first being the recognition of 12 uneven constellations along the ecliptic; followed by the division of the ecliptic into 12 equal proportions and culminating, circa 500 BC, in the still-used version of evenly distributed, 30-degree segments and signs. The Pumpsaint constellations are of uneven proportion and placement, which indicates that the temple's architecture was informed by the early-Babylonian era.

Crug y Biswal is partially enclosed by half a stone circle, which lends itself to have been a full circle before tarmac was laid upon old tracks approaching from the west and east, to form a road running alongside the tumulus. The overall appearance, today, suggests that some displaced stones were merely cast amongst the other remaining ones, to make way for the upgraded road.

The meaning and status of these ritual sites were such that they drew ancient green ways towards them, caused menhirs and marker stones to be erected and large lumps of white quartz to be carefully placed upon the elemental wilderness. So evocative and otherworldly had someone found this area to be, that it had compelled them to take down a municipal traffic sign and replace it with a warning-sign that fairies might be on the road.

❖ The fore of the outline of the ark takes in many of the ancestral funerary sites mentioned above. From Crug y Biswal, eastwards, the road is followed until it reaches a junction just to the west of Crug y Bwdran. Here a sharp right is taken and the route continues past Penygarreg, after which the detail of the outline becomes obscure.

- ❖ The rear of the outline of the ark is found by bearing westwards from Crug y Biswal and continuing to a junction of five roads, where a left turn onto the road to New Inn is followed. This road continues past Crug y Bedw, to a junction with a cairn on the other side of the road. Bearing right, the road quickly comes to a turning on the left, which is taken. From here, the route runs past Tirlan. However, I was unable to complete the final details of the outline and further dowsing work is needed.

The route, above, forms the outline of what Davies described as the "vessel without sails" which was pulled out of the waters by the sacred oxen of Hu. Through combining various bardic texts, he described that the *"naked vessel"* contained *"a male and female of every animal species"* from which the land was re-populated after the flooding of the *"Lake of Llion"*.

It is not difficult to imagine that it would be told that the survival of the inhabitants of the ark was miraculous; a merciful act of both the benign and powerful sun who had caused the flood-waters to recede and of the "genius of the vessel", or the force of wisdom and intuition, which had occupied and guided the vessel.

The safe landing of the ark; the setting of foot on earth once again and the regeneration of the species to follow, would all have evoked feelings of immense gratitude and veneration of the gods who had bestowed favour; not least, the sun god and his wife, Ceridwen.

8
Orion

Symbol: A man with club.

Ian Ridpath describes that Orion is portrayed by Homer, in 'Odyssey', as a hunter with a club of bronze.

In today's zodiac, Gemini and Cancer follow Taurus; in the Pumpsaint sanctuary, the constellations of Orion and Argo Navis are to be found instead. Thompson confirms that Orion and Gemini were both found within the same section of the ecliptic in the 5th century BC in Babylonia, so the hunter, Orion, is a reasonable substitute for the heavenly twins of Gemini.

Like Edwards, I have been unable to find an outline for Hydra, which is present in the Glastonbury zodiac; although Argo

Navis is represented in this temple as the ark behind Taurus, seen in Chapter 7. My results aren't definitive and it may be that Hydra and/or Gemini are yet to be discovered within the sanctuary. However, club-wielding Orion is in the appropriate sequence.

❖ At Maestyle, the line of Orion's back is formed by the lane to Brynbach.

❖ Just west of Maestyle is a lane which heads southwards past Bryniau-isaf and Bryniau-uchaf, delineating the trunk of Orion's body; it then swings westwards to Rhydcymerau, forming the legendary 'belt'.

❖ The path defining Orion's face is found by following a path to the east of Maestyle, across boggy land to Esgerwen and, then, bearing westwards until it reaches a tarmac land.

❖ The club of Orion is shaped, on one side, by a lane running north, north-westwards from Maestyle which passes through Wern, where an upright menhir stands prominently near the entrance to the farm. From Wern, the way becomes a rough track, laden with a sense of ancient mystery, as it continues north, north-westwards, onto Blaen-Ceiment and beyond to join a now-familiar crossroad of paths (co-shared by the outlines of Aries and Taurus), where it takes a left turn to Pantycrwys. The following is not mapped as a public footpath but, at Pantycrwys, the route follows the row of standing-stones, set side-by-side along a raised field-boundary on the left, and continues southwards, past Penybanc, until it joins a tarmac lane.

The remnants of a wall of standing stones at Pantycrwys brings to mind Aneurin's description of the "great stone fence of their common sanctuary", in his poem, 'Gododin', as translated by Davies. The name 'Pantycrwys' means 'hollow of the crosses'.

❖ All of Orion's outline is contained within the larger features of Taurus, apart from his legs; one of which follows the B4337 from Sunny Bank to just above Llethr Bledrig; and along the tranquil, antiquated 'green road' from Sunny Bank, past Banc Cwm-Hywel and Banc Cwm-coed-Ifor.

❖ The second leg is only partially visible; the top of which is created by following an old route from Orion's chin, to the left of Esgerwen, and continuing south-eastwards alongside woodland, until it touches the old green road. I didn't stop to check on the map whether this track was a right of way, only discovering later that it wasn't.

Robb describes that bronze and iron-age roads were well-constructed; highlighting that pre-Roman chariots were engineered with considerable sophistication and many were "delicately sprung", fine-wheeled, ornately adorned and certainly "not designed to run on rubbly, winding tracks". The sites of the Pumpsaint temple are well-served, and often inter-connected, by these ancient thoroughfares.

Many old, straight roads in Britain have been attributed to the work and skill of the Romans, but this idea is now challenged. Graham Robb notes that the so-called 'Roman' roads often took the shortest route between settlements but, at times, would veer off at a tangent to show "a curious attraction to a Celtic site". He proposes that the Romans took over and utilised ancient by-ways and that the reason the legions of Caesar could cover such daily distances in Gaul was because they didn't have to wait for the roads and bridges to be built first. A glance at any Welsh map shows how many 'Roman', but perhaps early Celtic, roads are still in existence.

9

Canes Minor

Symbol: A little dog

The position of Canes Minor in the night-sky is at the heels of Orion. In the Pumpsaint sanctuary, it is correspondingly located.

❖ The outline of Canes Minor is shaped by well-defined 'green' roads and footpaths through largely coniferous forestry. From Gwernogle, running south-eastwards past Clyn Wallis, a green path is taken to a footbridge, which is crossed to follow an incomplete track towards Pont Nant-y-ffin, giving shape to one side of the dog's tail and hindquarters.

❖ Taking a short path running north-westwards above Nant-y-ffin to a T-junction of tracks, the route is followed to Rhandir-gini and a fork in the paths. Here, a right-turn is taken along a path running past Esgairffordd and to the tarmac road at Abergorlech.

❖ A few yards eastwards, a well-defined green route running in a north-westerly direction from the forestry visitor's car-park in Abergorlech is taken to a fork in the paths at Banc Disgwylfa. Here, a right-turn is picked up, and is followed all the way through to Trawscoed to form the shape of the dog's face. The original shape of the ear is shown on the 1947 map (as portrayed above) but has been lost in recent times due to a re-routing of the footpath.

❖ At Trawscoed, the way leads towards Llettyllwynde to form the back of the dog's head, and continues along a tarmac lane to Pant-Yr-Eglwys (church of the hollow) and beyond. After the church, the second footpath on the right is taken, to Gwernogle; creating the shape of the dog's back and top of its tail.

Llanfihangel Church at Pant-Yr-Eglwys is situated in a lonely spot and has the hallowed atmosphere of a spiritual sanctuary; its placement, set within a temple landscape of a Celtic belief system, does not seem at all incongruent.

Canon Thomas' notes reveal that, for centuries, Pant-yr-Eglwys stood on a ring-shaped site dating back to the pre-Christian era. The current churchyard wall, with its striking upper layer of white quartz stones, was built after 1900.

When I visited, the church was locked. Wandering outside, I came across a labyrinth in an enclosure to the right-hand side of the churchyard. Walking along the curves, twists and turns towards the still-point of the centre, I was able to reflect on the much larger journey that initiates would have taken through the different symbols of the Pumpsaint Temple of the Stars. Almost certainly, it would have been a demanding, difficult and transformative experience.

Davies described that great bravery was required of the trainee Druids; initiation was hard-won; and rightly so. The courage each initiate had to find within themselves was a demonstration that they were going to be able to fulfil their Druidic remit with honour and integrity. The Druids were the priests and judges of the early Celts and they were esteemed for conducting their offices with morality and wisdom.

Canon Thomas posed that Llanfihangel Church had been built on the site of an ancient cemetery. This is in keeping with Allcroft's findings that the Celts buried their dead within circles and that, where the church took over pre-Christian sacred sites, the circular Celtic burial grounds became circular graveyards; some of which were later straightened out.

Circles were a sacred representation of all aspects of life to the Celts; the burial mound, the forest grove and the stone circle were all sanctified spaces in which they performed rites and acts of worship. In parallel with nature's eternally revolving seasons, circles symbolised a belief in the everlasting human cycle of birth, life, death and re-birth. Moreover, 'circles' represent the feminine principle, whereas the linear 'cross' symbolises an era of masculine spirituality.

The early Celtic crosses which incorporate both the images of a circle and a cross, as well as the circular Christian graveyards which housed a rectangular church building, speak of a transitional time between the old religion founded on mother-nature herself, and the new patriarchal faith.

Canon Thomas recorded that the first church to be established at Pant-yr-Eglwys was a chapel-of-ease, replacing a hermit's cell which dated back to the 6th or 7th century AD; a time when, according to the bards, there were vehement attempts to overthrow their sacred sites and, by implication, the heart of their old religion.

In medieval times, the church was a place of pilgrimage. On catching first sight of Pant-yr-Eglwys, the pilgrims would kneel on a large stone (reportedly, still there in the 1940's) in a field known as 'Cae'r Paderau Bach' (the field of little prayers); there, they offered prayers of thanks for their safe arrival. Over the centuries, then, the pull of this hallowed ground; the value of an arduous journey and the recognition of a stone's worth, were shared by Druids and Christians alike at Pant-yr-Eglwys, transcending religious ideology.

The parish is dedicated to Archangel Michael (in Welsh, SantMihangel) who, it was believed, had the power to dispel unwanted forces from the past. Canon Thomas tells of a legend in which, initially, the church was to be built at Penygarreg; inexplicably, however, each night the day's building work was undone. Eventually, the stonemason gave up and threw his hammer with fury, announcing that wherever it fell would be the new ground upon which he would build. It was an Olympian throw and landed at Pant-yr-Eglwys.

As with many old myths, there is a likely grain of truth in the story. Penygarreg is sited on the outline of the sacred ark, the area containing burial mounds of the most prominent and revered of the early Celts. Attempts to take over such a sacrosanct part of the temple would, presumably, elicit nothing less than resolute resistance from the Druids, who may have quietly dismantled the newly erected church walls under the cover of the night, in order to avoid open conflict and disruption within the community. It is possible to imagine that, with great sorrow, they may have acquiesced to the usurpation of their sacred site at Pant-yr-Eglwys, in order to protect the most hallowed ground of their ancestors.

10

Cancer

Symbol: A crab

Lewis Edwards concluded that Orion and Argo Navis were to be found as substitutes for both Gemini and Cancer, in the Pumpsaint zodiac; however, I have found the sign of Cancer to be clearly defined in this temple.

- ❖ The extended claw of cancer is delineated by a high ridge-path, starting from just below Blaen-y-cwm, where it leads over a stile on the left of the track and drops west, south-westwards down to Ffynnonau.

Here, the open views across rolling countryside are magnificent. Walking the ridge in this direction at the end of a clear late-autumn day, the skies were ablaze with an eruption of fiery and inky sunset colours as light gave way to the hushed beauty of a chilly, starlit night.

❖ Again, starting from just below Blaen-y-cwm, the other side of the claw is formed by following the track which bears directly westwards, before taking a footpath on the left to Blaennant and continuing on to Talley.

Talley, itself, is home to the picturesque ruins of an abbey of the 12th century. It was established for the order of the 'White Canons' (officially known as the Premonstratensians) and is situated next to two lakes. The monks' activities, of farming fish and working the arable land attached to the monastery, enabled them to support themselves.

Parker and Petersen describe that Cancer is symbolized as a crab, crayfish, or lobster. Interestingly, there are two possible versions of cancer in the Pumpsaint zodiac, a crayfish and a crab. They have many shared features, covering much of the same area.

❖ The outline of the body of the crayfish follows a track which can be picked up by leaving Talley on the road running south to Cwmdu and taking the first footpath on the right, which skirts the edge of Allt yr Arian, bearing westwards.

❖ From Allt yr Arian, the route runs along the south side of Mynydd Cynros until it reaches the road above Blaenwaun.

❖ The fuller outline of the crab follows the lane, north-west at Talley, around to Cilyllynfawr and on to Blaenwaun.

❖ At Blaenwaun, the outline, as it returns to Talley, is shared by both the crab and the crayfish and is formed by following a path to Cwmyryn and eastwards to Penybryn, then curving southwards to Ffos-las. At Ffos-las, the path runs westwards to join the lane to Halfway. Just before reaching the main road at Halfway, a right of way on the left returns to Talley.

Both versions of Cancer were significant when dowsed and this has led me to consider that the Temple constellation-sites may have been updated as the discipline of astronomy evolved. Robb's book, 'The Ancient Paths', provides examples of the numerous ways in which Druids developed and utilised knowledge and it is, therefore, likely that their openness to emerging ideas would have been reflected in alterations of the structure of the temple, over time.

On this theme, Davies revealed that the Druids had little problem integrating Christian ideas into their existing belief system, saying "when the bards became acquainted with scripture history, they perceived, and frequently alluded to, the connection between their own national traditions, and the sacred records, respecting Noah and his family. Hence they considered their own . . . . as not absolutely irreconcilable with Christianity."

However, it appears that the Christian church didn't see things in quite the same way and Davies gave account that Christian burial was sometimes refused "to these Gentile priests".

11

Leo

Symbol: A lion

Leo was one of the earlier identified constellations. Much symbolism has been attributed to the lion across the ages; its image is taken to represent the radiant, light aspect of the sun. In 'A Guide to Glastonbury's Temple of the Stars', Maltwood told that the Druid chief of Britain was referred to as a lion; and the lion was also an important symbol in the Roman system of Mithra.

❖ The outline is incomplete. However, taking the small road running northwards, from Llansawel, the front of the hind leg is formed. After a while, a lane on the right, to Pistyllgwyn, is taken. After the farm there, the route becomes an ancient track with a few surviving beech trees alongside.

❖ Continuing, the way comes to a fork and both directions are significant; a right-turn to Gareg, and another right within 'Brechfa forest' where the path forks again, leads past Tan-y-lan and onto Pantydderwen, forming the underbelly of Leo and the back of one of the fore-legs.

❖ However, after Pistyllgwyn, if a northwards direction is chosen at the fork, a quartz-strewn track with raised banks, reaches Banc Pistyll-gwyn, giving shape to the hind leg before continuing up towards the back and mane of the Leo outline.

This invigorating old way crosses airy and open grassland. Here, much of the path has been almost cultivated out of existence, but not quite; evidence remains in a visible, slightly raised crease at the edge of the curved track and there are occasional lumps of white quartz at the fence-line, which runs alongside.

❖ After a while, passing a tumulus on the left, the route reaches a crossroad of four paths; a right-turn south-westwards, later curving north-westwards to Hafodymaidd and on to Glanyrafon, forms the lower part of Leo's mane.

❖ Straight ahead at the crossroad, the path reaches Maesdy, joins a tarmac road and continues on to Rhosgoch and beyond, to create the outline of Leo's back and shoulders. After Rhosgoch, the route briefly joins the main A482, east, south-eastwards, before turning left into a lane; quickly after, the first footpath on the right is taken, in the direction of Llwynrhos.

❖ At Llwynrhos, the route of the outline joins the old Roman road, southwards, very briefly, before it turns left along a lane to Henllan, which eventually returns to the A482; resulting in the head of Leo being defined.

❖ Taking a left-turn at the earlier crossroad of paths above the marked tumulus, a quartz-strewn track leads westwards down to Groes. At Groes, the route briefly joins the road to Llansawel, before picking up a track on the right to Bryndafydd-uchaf and turning left through the woods to Tan-y-coed and beyond to form the hind quarters of Leo.

❖ After reaching Tan-y-coed, a track on the other side of the Afon Marlais is visible. It has three large recumbent stones and a double-row of oaks leading down to the water. However, the day I was there, the river was in full spate and I was unable to cross.

❖ A couple of weeks later, I returned to the Llansawel area, picking up a route at Sunny Bank which headed northwards past Glynmarch, after which it curved north-westwards, before almost doubling up on itself, turning sharply eastwards. Unsure if this was now private land and feeling strangely uneasy, I retraced my steps. The route may have led to the crossing near Tan-y-coed to form the back of Leo's hind-leg, but it remains unverified.

❖ The front of Leo's chest and rear of one of Leo's fore-legs is formed by a lane running south-eastwards from the bottom of Leo's head, at Glanyrafon, as it skirts the eastern edge of Allt Penarth and runs down past Cefntelych Lodge and onwards to Penny. At Penny, a left-turn is taken onto the main road and a bridge over Afon Cothi is crossed, before picking up a right turn across a field to the 'Twrla Stone'. Here, the route changes direction, heading northwards, to form the front foot of Leo and the front of one of the fore-legs.

The Twrla Stone, itself, lays recumbent near to what appears to be a man-made, steep-sided mound. On first visit, the stone and mound were found in a small cover of pine trees, which kept the ground relatively clear of undergrowth. Returning recently, a few years later, the trees were dead and the land had been taken over by thick scrub, concealing the stone and softening the steep-sided conical shape of the mound.

In Allcroft's work, 'The Circle and the Cross', it is explained that the early Celts would gather at a mound to conduct matters of law. This meeting place was referred to as a 'moot' and was also the place of other communal activities and rituals.

Allcroft described that Druidism was a well-organised administrative, political and educational system and that:

"The ultimate virtue aimed at by the *druidical disciplina* was justice. The druids were the justices of their time. As nothing was done without their intervention they must have been accessible . . . there must have been druids in every community where the system was prevalent; for every community of necessity had its own moot".

An advantage of the mound was that the community leaders could be seen by those gathered below; perhaps, too, these mounds offered status, symbolically raising the Druids above the crowd. A different explanation might be that, to the Celts, high places were associated with being closer to the heavens; from the mounds, then, the Druids would be better placed to receive spiritual wisdom as they conducted their role as judge, priest or celebrant.

The true purpose of the mound in the sign of Leo has long been lost. However, 'twr' means 'heap' in the Welsh language and this heap was once esteemed enough to warrant a standing stone to be placed next to it.

12

Virgo

Symbol: A woman brandishing a sheaf of corn

The landscape contained within Virgo's generously proportioned body has a timeless, deeply rural, unspoilt quality and covers a mix of undulating countryside, quiet hamlets and criss-crossing footpaths; along with sections of straight, single-track road; marsh land and occasional farmsteads. Her voluptuousness indicates that she is fertile, providing, nurturing and sustaining. She is mother earth.

❖ The outline of Virgo's body runs from Talley to Caio, where it shapes the back of her head. From Caio, a right turn to Aberbowlan creates detail of Virgo's bonnet, where another right turn to Pont-yr-Efail forms the outline of her face. A left turn at Pont-yr-Efail, turning south towards Llanwrda, marks out the front of Virgo's body.

❖ Virgo's wheat-sheaf is delineated by setting off from Caio, where the white-quartz topped churchyard wall exudes a sense of bygone spiritual significance. On the day I visited, heading north, north-eastwards through Caeo Forest, I found there was a pervasive feeling of antiquity despite the unnatural, dark blanket of conifer and eerie howls from somewhere deep within the gloom; which turned out to be no more than the cries of a stray foxhound.

❖ Before long, the route emerged from the forest and climbed up to the course of an old Roman aqueduct and along a green lane to the hillside above Cwrt-y-cadno. Here the direction of the outline changed, taking a right-turn and climbing up an old track until it reached a point where it is crossed by another path, just before the edge of Mynydd Mallaen. Turning right along the path running towards the southwest, the upper part of the wheat-sheaf is formed.

❖ The whole wheat-sheaf outline is created by continuing straight ahead to the next crossroad in the tracks, where the path on the right towards Rhyd Ddu is taken, quickly followed by a further right-turn, back through Caeo forest. In the forest, this path is crossed by another, delineating some more of the outline of Virgo's bonnet.

In the zodiac, Virgo is often represented brandishing a sheaf of corn. According to Davies' translations, the celestial temples of the Welsh Druids were used for the rites and worship of Ceres or Ceridwen.

That Roman Ceres should be honoured by the Druids in their temple confirms their openness to other cultures and religions. In doing so, perhaps the Druids exhibited diplomacy and wisdom; ensuring that the Romans would be more likely to accept their practices without hostile interference.

Davies indicated that the Romans allowed the Celts some degree of self-governance and that, especially as the Romans would have been unable to understand their spoken language, the Druids "would naturally preserve the memory of their sacred poems and traditional institutes: they would also continue to perform their mystical rites".

The bard, Cuhelyn, described Celtic Ceridwen as "the goddess of various seeds". Similarly, Ceres was the Roman goddess of corn and Davies concluded that Ceres was synonymous with Ceridwen and, in fact, any female deity around the world "in whom are personified the generative powers", such as Venus, Rhea and Selene; she is "the common parent, the mother of all humankind".

In 'The Golden Bough', Frazer gave a comprehensive account of rituals held throughout the world in honour of this fruitful earth-goddess at the time of the corn-harvest. In Britain, the 'harvest festival' is a remnant of the Celtic tradition of celebration and thankfulness to the deity of the corn-crop and, to this day, 'corn-dollies' are woven and brought indoors over winter, keeping old customs alive.

From very ancient times, the great feminine deity was revered as a 'triple aspect' goddess. She was maiden, mother and crone with a corresponding connection to the phases of the moon - crescent, full and dark.

Between the symbol of Virgo-as-mother and Libra, two other aspects of the triune goddess can be found.

❖ The maiden's face and head are formed by small lanes and rights of way from Porthrhyd to Poley and to Aberbowlan; then, westwards to Blaen-dyffryn, Pencraig, Benlan and back to Porthrhyd.

The image of 'mother and maiden-child' in the temple is touchingly tender, portraying the beneficence and creative power of this nature-deity; along with a joyful celebration of new life.

X

The hook-nosed, cackling crone is holding aloft a burning torch. She is positioned to the east of Llandovery, north of the A40. Her eye and teeth are my own additions, to better define her features.

- ❖ Her face is formed by following country roads from Llanwrda to Llwyncellyn and northwards to a junction where a left turn to Bwlch-y-gwynt is taken and, then, north-westwards to Troedrhiwresger.

- ❖ At the same junction, a right turn to Cwm-Myns-isaf and northwards to Cwmargenau, Cwmto-fawr and Trebannau depicts the fore of the crone's arm and the torch and flame.

- ❖ In parallel, from Glyncoch, then northwards past Cwm-Mynys to Rhiwrhwch Isaf and on to Trebannau, the rear of her arm, torch and flame are outlined.

The crone-aspect of the goddess symbolises the dark moon and the concealed, unpredictable, terrifying or destructive qualities of the feminine principle in nature. The flame of her burning torch, a female image, is formed by old green ways and boggy sunken tracks; as with a figure of eight, its shape is without beginning or end. It is akin to an elaborate 'mandorla'.

To the Celts, the 'eternal flame' symbolised the light of the moon and was often tended by women of the temples. In the Welsh sanctuary, however, Davies translated that a man was keeper of the 'eternal flame' and that his wife was associated with the mysteries. Her name was 'Bun'.

A 'mandorla' is the almond shape formed by two overlapping circles and has many meanings attached to it, including the coming together of opposite qualities which, through their union, result in a numinous place of transformation. This 'mandorla' is formed not by circles, but by what appear to be two overlapping oak-leaf shapes.

There is at least one more oak-leaf shape within the temple, which will be described later. In itself, it should not be surprising to find depictions of oak leaves within the sanctuary; Druids have long been associated with the oak tree. While the origins of the name 'Druid' are unknown, one theory is that it derives from the Celtic word for oak, 'dru'.

As highlighted by Graham Robb, Celtic coins often displayed a head of the Greek sun-god, adorned with a wreath of oak leaves; and Pliny described that the Druids planted oak-groves and their leaves had been a feature in all of their sacred ceremonies.

13

Libra

Symbol: A dove

The constellation of Libra was excluded from the zodiac by
the Babylonians, who saw it as being the claws of Scorpio.
The symbol we have today is a pair of scales and it was re-
introduced by the Romans; the scales represent 'balance'.

In the Pumpsaint Sanctuary, there are no scales; however, an
outline of a bird, possibly a dove, can be found in its place.
At first, I was inclined to dismiss this finding, until I read in
Maltwood's account that, likewise, in the Glastonbury land-
zodiac, there were no scales to be found in the position of
Libra, but a dove.

❖ The outline of the dove covers an undulating,
    peaceful landscape found to the north-west of
    Llandovery. The shape of the wing is formed by a

lane running north-westwards from Maes yr Haf, which quickly curves south-westwards and then north-westwards again along the edge of Banc Cae-glas. At Banc Cae-glas, the route turns north-easterly, past Penybanc Uchaf and onwards to a T-junction.

❖ At the T-Junction, a right-turn south, south-westwards along a green right of way, leads past Trebannau to Wern, to form the back of the bird. The bird's tail is shaped by continuing south-westwards, past Cwmto-fawr and Allt-yr-adar-fach, before turning eastwards to the bottom of Allt Rhiw'r hwch Isaf, and then north, north-eastwards along the valley to Rhiwrhwch Isaf.

❖ At Rhiwrhwch Isaf, the route follows a wavy lane eastwards to Allt Rhiw'r hwch Uchaf and then north, north-eastwards past Bwlchmaenllwyd to Cefn-trenfa. This forms the front of the bird's body.

❖ At Cefn-trenfa, continuing northwards, the route reaches a crossroad. Here, a left-turn westwards is taken, past Gilwen and Pen-y-groes to a further T-junction, where a left-turn south, south-westwards delineates the head as it re-joins the outline of the bird's back.

In the story of the ark, after the deluge had ceased a dove was set free from the boat and returned with evidence of dry land.

14

Scorpio

Symbol: An eagle

The constellation, Aquila the Eagle, is found in the house of Scorpio and has long been seen in place of the more commonly used image for Scorpio, the scorpion.

Mesocosm describes that on an ancient portal artefact from Assyria, known as the 'guardian' of the palace of Nimrud, dating from around 965 BC, the celestial constellations associated with the equinoxes and solstices are displayed. In that era, these astronomical annual events occurred in the signs of Taurus, Scorpio, Leo and Aquarius, which were depicted on the 'guardian' by a bull, eagle, lion and human figure, respectively.

Later, around 600 BC, Ezekiel referred to this 'tetramorph', these four creatures in the heavens, saying:

"As for the likeness of their faces, they four had the faces of a man, and the face of a lion, on the right side; and they four had the face of an ox on the left side; they four also had the face of an eagle".

Dowsing for the sign of Scorpio was initially baffling. On each attempt, the rod took me away from the suggested route above Cwrt-y-Cadno and created lines on the map that were clearly not going to form themselves into the scorpion-image I expected to find. Eventually, I made a note of the partial findings and decided to focus on a different site for a while.

When I did return to the matter of Scorpio, I had already concluded that I should abandon preconceived ideas and just follow the rods to see what emerged. Map-dowsing gave an indication I should begin from the village of Cilycwm.

The listed St Michael's church at Cilycwm is unusual, with old paintings on the south wall, which Caroe describes as originating from the 18th century. Cornah tells that while the building dates from around the 13th or 14th century, the churchyard site is far more ancient, with one of its yews being over 1500 years old. The church, itself, has stones of white quartz built into its structure.

On the west wall is a painted figure of death; a crude skeletal figure with a spear. In astrology, death is associated with the sign of Scorpio and, to the Celts, the west was the place of the ancestors. This image could indicate that attachment to symbols of the old religion persisted for a considerable time in this part of Wales.

Almost certainly, the move from Celtic to Christian belief was unlikely to have been achieved in a clean moment of transition; but the representation of death on the west wall of the church at Cilycwm gives rise to the possibility that the clergy, themselves, were partially orientated to the Celtic ways or, at least, were willing to appease their parishioners in these matters.

Dowsing from Cilycwm took place over several days; gradually, it became apparent that the outline of an eagle, not a scorpion, had been etched upon the earth as a representation of Scorpio.

❖ To form the outline of the body of the eagle, a northwards direction out of Cilycwm is followed. Soon, an old green track on the left is taken, running westwards past Glangwenlais. It climbs steeply to the mountain-land of Rhiw Cilgwyn, above Cwm Merchon (valley of the women). At Rhiw Cilgwyn, there is a track which turns steeply downhill to the left; it forms the front of the fore-leg of the eagle, but is not the route to be followed at present.

❖ Heading westwards at Rhiw Cilgwyn and, then, north-westwards along the footpath which runs across Esgair Ferchon (ridge of the women), the lower part of the eagle's fore-wing is completed as the track turns northwards past Rhyd Ddu.

❖ After Rhyd Ddu, the route bears left, westwards, past Rhiw Garegog to just above Cwrt-y-Cadno. Here a left-turn is taken, along the old green track to Llwyn-y-ceiliog, where a right turn follows the lane to Cwrt-y-Cadno. Just beyond Cwrt-y-Cadno, in a north-easterly direction, is a small footpath on the right which, if taken, returns to the bridge across the tumbling Afon Cothi. This completes the outline of the lower part of the eagle's head and the whole beak.

❖ The upper head and far-wing of the eagle is formed by following this beautiful river valley along the quiet country road from Cwrt-y-Cadno to Bwlch-y-rhiw, heading in a north-easterly direction. At Bwlch-y-rhiw, the route curves eastwards and then south-eastwards until it skirts around Allt Pwll-priddog in a south-westerly direction briefly, before taking a right-turn along the footpath leading up to Mynydd Mallaen.

❖ Instead, of bearing right to Mynydd Mallaen, the complete outline of the fore-wing is formed by taking a left-turn along a footpath, across Afon Twyi and then a right-turn along a green track to Gwernpwll. After Gwernpwll, a right-turn onto the lane is taken, southwards past Clynmawr, before the route takes a right-turn at a fork in the road, heading in a north-westerly direction past Rhydfelen. Just after Ty-newydd, the footpath straight-ahead is taken. It runs beneath Cae'r-beili, back towards Glangwenlais.

- ❖ Mynydd Mallaen has traces of its spiritual significance still present, marked with an occasional lump of white quartz and a standing stone to the right, as it takes a westerly route to distinguish one wing from the other.

- ❖ After the standing stone has been reached, the track soon divides and the two paths delineate the eagle's wings from its head.

- ❖ Taking the left branch of the track, which runs above Banc y Ddau Fryn, across Pen Cerrigdiddos, to a crossroad in the path, delineates the fore-wing from the eagle's head.

- ❖ Taking the right branch of the fork, however, the route passes by another standing stone on the right, Maen Bach, and leads down the mountainside, past Crugiau Merched (graves of the Women), to the small, white-washed Baptist chapel of Bwlchyrhiw, which is nestled between the steep slopes and the river. Nearby, are the remains of an open-air baptismal pool filled by the icy waters of the north-facing mountain-stream, Gog-yr-nant.

It is notable that the graves, a valley and a mountain-ridge on Mynydd Mallaen are all identified as women's sites. Crugiau Merched dates back to the bronze-age, a time before the construction of the temple. There are many bronze-age monuments within the sanctuary and Robb describes that the Druids esteemed ancestral sites and intentionally made use of them at times. It is likely, then, that Crugiau Merched would have been honoured by the later Druid architects of the Pumpsaint sanctuary.

- ❖ The outline of the front of the fore-leg is formed by returning to the climb up to Rhiw Cilgwyn from Glangwenlais, then dropping down from Rhiw Cilgwyn, in a south, south-easterly direction, along the marked green road on the left. When the way reaches a crossroad, continue straight ahead to just west of Pen-y-groes until a fork is reached, whereupon a left-turn is taken.

- ❖ The back of the fore-leg, and the demarcation between the two legs, is formed by a lane just to the east of Glangwenlais, running southwards through Cilycwm to Cefn-trenfa, just after which, it bears right along a footpath.

- ❖ The outline of the back of the eagle's rear leg is formed by finding the bottom of the eagle's wing at its tail-end. There, bearing north-westwards, past Rhydfelen and over the bridge which crosses Afon Twyi, the route takes an immediate left onto a footpath running south, past Penlan and Aberdunant, where it briefly follows the course of Afon Twyi, before it reaches a junction at Pont Newydd. The route then takes a right turn westwards, before it curves southwards along a lane running past Erryd House, Erryd and Erryd Wood.

The Cilycwm history group explains that 'Erydd' is derived from the Welsh word 'eryr' and one of its various meanings is 'eagle'. Additionally, the word can mean 'chief' or 'prince' and also refers to the symbol of an eagle on a Roman standard. To the ancients, the eagle was a highly-esteemed bird, laden with symbolic meaning.

15

Gryphon

Symbol: A gryphon (also, 'griffin' or 'griffon')

The image of a gryphon began to emerge while I was dowsing in the sign of Sagittarius, in Llanddewi-Brefi. Unexpectedly, the rod indicated the significance of a road and I could see from the map that this route led to some interesting ancient sites; with investigations completed in Llanddewi-Brefi for the day, I decided to follow the rod's lead.

> ❖ Heading out of Llanddewi-Brefi, in a south-eastwards direction, the gently-climbing green mountain-valley

with its wild brooks of Afon Brefi and Afon Pysgotwr were compelling. Just after Pysgotwr, at Nant-gwernog, two pertinent routes were indicated; a green road on the right, and a stony lane straight ahead.

❖ Continuing ahead, the track climbs up to the remote beauty of spectacular mountain-land, which is eventually punctuated by a standing stone on the right; soon after, the path plunges dramatically down towards Troed-rhiw-cymmer and sporadic habitation. At the time, looking only for zodiac signs, I was unable to see the relevance of the map-lines formed. However, the findings were noted and put to one side. Only much later did I understand that this track created the shape of the front of the gryphon's wing. *Include [*
p 79 -

❖ At Troed-rhiw-cymmer, the way continues past Troed-rhiw-ruddwen, bearing southwards briefly, before crossing the river on the right, to Rhydygroes. Here, an immediate left turn, along a footpath running south-eastwards, is taken; it curves around Allt Maesmeddygon, before the route follows a path crossing Craig Alltyberau, to Gallt-y-bere. At Gallt-y-bere, it crosses the river-bridge and completes the face of the gryphon.

❖ The area around Troed-rhiw-ruddwen is mystical. From Troed-rhiw-ruddwen, heading southwards and turning right at Rhydygroes, a track is followed towards the gryphon's ear; there it curves eastwards up to Allt Penrhiw-iar and back around to Troed-rhiw-ruddwen, creating the shape of a star on the gryphon's forehead.

Outside the sign of the gryphon, but worth noting, is a track leading north-eastwards from Troed-rhiw-ruddwen, up towards Llyn Brianne. Near the top, slightly to the right of the track, is a small, unmapped white-quartz standing stone, with rocks and pieces of white-quartz and rose-quartz, clustered together nearby, in a miniature cairn-like fashion; creating an overall impression of a gentle and peaceful shrine, amidst a rugged landscape.

❖ The fore of the Gryphon is shaped by taking a westwards turn at Rhandirmwyn itself, to the church, where a green-road on the left, running past the sewage works, is followed alongside the river, which it crosses, before it joins a footpath leading westwards to Mynydd Mallaen.

❖ Continuing up to Mynydd Mallaen, the gryphon's body is outlined by the same ancient track with quartz stones and a standing stone that delineates one eagle's wing from another in Scorpio, before it bears right past Maen Bach and the little church at Bwlch-y-rhiw. At Bwlch-y-rhiw, the route heads eastwards towards Troed-y-rhiw-dinas.

❖ At Troed-y-rhiw-dinas, a left-turn is taken and, then, right across the river where a quick left-turn is taken, up along a boundary, past another standing stone on the left, after which, it reaches a crossroad of tracks and the left-hand route heads north-westwards along the green-road back to Pysgotwr, completing the shape of the gryphon's wing. To the right, the path forks and runs north-eastwards to outline the top of the gryphon's ear and head; or south-eastwards to form the bottom of the gryphon's ear and, then, southwards to define its neck.

❖ The route back to Pysgotwr passes the stone circle on Pen-y-raglan-wynt, on the left. Map-dowsing suggests that a parallel track on the west side of the circle may form another wing. It is included in the diagram above, but needs further research.

The Glastonbury Temple of the Stars contains the image of a gryphon. In her book, Katherine Maltwood described that the Roman temple at Caerleon, in South Wales, was dedicated to the worship of Mithra and she relayed that, according to the system of Mithra, a gryphon "watched over mines of gold and hidden treasure"; this is in keeping with more ancient mythologies.

Given that many legends have substance and, within this celestial sanctuary, gold mines were worked by people from both the bronze-age and the Roman-era, as well the fact that *reward* a store of gold treasure was found in the 18th century, it seemed possible that a gryphon might be incorporated within the overall temple area. When the search for the constellation sites was almost complete, an empty area *transfer to p. 77* between Scorpio and Sagittarius stood out; it was the place I had been led to dowse a few years earlier and further investigations were indicated.

The gryphon is a very ancient, mythological symbol of Eastern origin; variously depicted as a terrifying and

79

ferocious combination of lion and eagle. In many images, they have well-defined ears as they are reputed to have astonishing powers of hearing. John Vinycomb, in 'Fictitious and Symbolic creatures in Art', quoted Sir Thomas Browne's portrayal of a gryphon as "Emblematical of watchfulness, courage, perseverance and rapidity of execution".

A two-inch, gold, flying gryphon found by Dr Schliemann in the ancient bronze-age city of Mycenae has lion-paws, rather than the usual extended eagle talons; the Pumpsaint gryphon shares this feature.

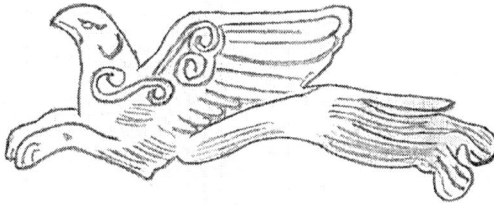

Sketch of two-inch, gold, flying gryphon found in ancient city of Mycenae.

Robb describes that the gateway to Druidic sites is often in the north-east. If he is correct, then the Pumpsaint gryphon would have been a fearsome sentry placed to guard the entrance of the sacred sanctuary. With a defined ear and single prominent star emblazoned over its 'third-eye', the gryphon of this temple might have symbolised an all-hearing, far-seeing creature; one imbued with magical and formidable powers of guardianship and protection.

16

Sagittarius

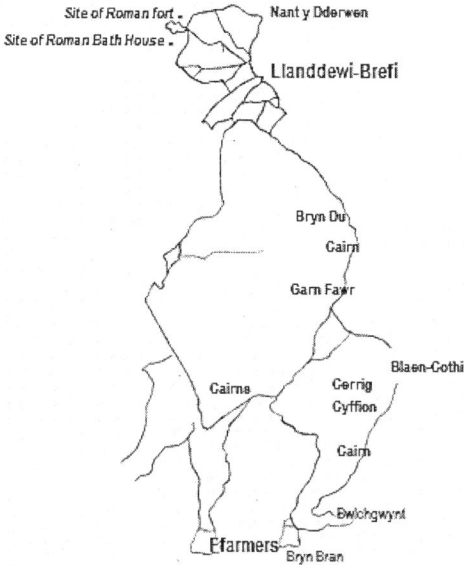

Site of Roman fort ▪
Site of Roman Bath House ▪
Nant y Dderwen
Llanddewi-Brefi
Bryn Du
Cairn
Garn Fawr
Blaen-Cothi
Cairns
Cerrig Cyffion
Cairn
Bwlchgwynt
Ffarmers
Bryn Bran

Symbol: Half warrior, half horse

Sagittarius is usually depicted as half-human, half horse. In traditional astrology, the human part of the image is often an archer; here, it is depicted as a soldier of the iron-age.

The symbol of Sagittarius is incomplete; markedly, the horse's tail is missing and, possibly, there is a cape flying behind the figure. These are areas needing further investigation.

- ❖ The horse's saddle is shaped by following a lane running west of Blaen-Twrch, before taking the first left and the first left again to Wernfeudwy; then north, north-eastwards back to Blaen-Twrch.

- ❖ The horse's hindquarters are defined by a boundary-wall leading eastwards from Blaen-Twrch, curving south-eastwards to Blaen-Cothi and south, south-westwards past Cerrig Cyffion. Continuing in this direction, from Cerrig Cyffion to Blaenau, the shape of a hind leg starts to form.

- ❖ The rear hoof is created by taking an eastwards direction at Blaenau, along a lane, until the road turns in a south-easterly direction to a footpath on the right. This footpath is followed to Garth; shortly after this it reaches a fork.

- ❖ The left fork southwards leads to a green-road running westwards; this is followed to Bryn-Bran. At Bryn-Bran, taking a northerly direction, the path leads to Tyn-ddol, crossing an attractive small ford over Nant y Garth, to form the outline of the horse's hoof.

- ❖ The right-hand path of the fork, leads northwards to Tyn-ddol, where it joins the lane and continues north, north-easterly past Bryn Villa and Tynant, to the end. This completes the horse's rear leg.

- ❖ Where the lane ends, a footpath running west, north-westwards is followed. When it reaches the road just above Sychnant, a left-turn is taken, heading westwards and then southwards, all the way to Ffarmers; forming the rear of a foreleg and hoof.

- ❖ At Ffarmers, a right-turn westwards is followed by a right-turn north, north-eastwards until the road reaches a T-junction. By continuing up the lane, to Bwlch Blaen-corn which lies at the edge of an invigorating and precipitous landscape, the outline of one of the horse's forelegs is shaped.

- ❖ The other foreleg is not so clearly defined but, at Bwlch Blaen-corn, a short footpath running westwards is taken, followed by a left-turn onto the road to Cefnbryn, to form part of it.

- ❖ The front of this foreleg runs roughly parallel, to the west, and is shaped by following a footpath north, north-eastwards from just below Pantigwyn which joins a lane above Pant-yr-pistyll. At Pant-yr-pistyll a boundary wall westwards separates the leg from part of the cloak worn by the rider of the horse.

- ❖ The front of the human outline is defined by locating Sarn Helen, below the cairns on Esgair Fraith, to the right of Esgair-ddu. From here, heading north, north-westwards, the route continues to Pretoria. At Pretoria a right-turn is taken, curving around to Troed-y-bryn and then northwards to a T-junction between Pont Glanrhyd and Tan-yr-esgair. This section forms the front of a cloak.

❖ The outline of the soldier's lower arm is formed by
taking a right-turn at this T-junction and following
the lane eastwards. The upper arm is created by
turning left at the T-junction, over Pont Glanrhyd,
after which a footpath on the right, which runs
beneath Bryn Cysegrfa, is taken. This path joins a
lane and continues in a north-easterly direction to
Pengelli'r Bryn; it is then followed to Esgair-garn and
beyond, along old narrow roads, full of a sense of
mystery and with occasional small, upright stones
marking a field or hedge boundary, here and there.

❖ The head and neck of the soldier is armour-covered
and is made up of several clearly defined footpaths
in, and around, Llanddewi-Brefi. For the outline, the
footpath leading from Llanddewi-Brefi, south-
eastwards to Pentre-rhiw and beyond, is followed;
this path joins a lane turning north-westwards to
Ochrfod.

❖ At Ochrfod, the route takes a steep path down to
Talfan, turning north-eastwards past Tanrallt and
then to the B4343, where it turns right and left onto
a footpath running past Llwyn to Garth. Here the
way runs close to the Afon Teifi, past Godre'r-garth,
Ystrad-Dewi and Pont Llanio. From Pont Llanio, a
track shown on the 1947 map, to Nant-y-Dderwen, is
relevant but is no longer a right of way. From Nant-
y-Dderwen, the B4343 is taken, southwards, back to
Llanddewi-Brefi.

There is much lore attached to the church at Llanddewi-Brefi.
The town's history website, based on information compiled

by pupils and the headmaster of the local school in the 1970's, tells that the building is of the 12th century and was constructed on a pre-existing, raised, bronze-age mound. However, in folklore, the site's elevation was attributed to a miraculous event brought about by St David, who laid a cloth on the ground, causing it to rise up and lift him above the clamour of theological debate being held at the time, so that he could be heard.

Pertinently, Edward Davies described that "the religious seminary" at "Brevi" may have been founded on a sanctuary dedicated to the "rites of Hu and his oxen" and that, rather than the church replacing memories and symbolism of the old tradition, as intended, the founding bishop of St David's church, Dewi, merely became linked with the sacred bulls of the sun god. Davies demonstrated that this association persisted into the 12th century, at least; quoting the bard, Gwynfardd Brecheiniog:

"the oxen of Dewi, majestic were they. With equal pace, they moved to the festival. When they hastened, in conducting the sacred boon. . . Let us call upon God and Dewi, the two leaders of hosts, who, at this hour, willingly sojourn amongst us".

The church is home to a 6th to 9th century collection of Celtic crosses and stones. Given the legend that a standing stone on Bryn Cysegrfa was removed to Llanddewi-Brefi, perhaps these stones, too, were once plundered from the ancient temple-sanctuary of Pumpsaint.

❖ Returning to the outline of Sagittarius, the chest and shoulders of the warrior are formed by following the

85

lane northwards from Esgair-garn to Ochrfod. The back of the human is defined by taking a right-turn just above Ochrfod and following the road south-eastwards. This road was closed to vehicles when I visited, having fallen into serious disrepair; but the route continued through coniferous forestry, with the uncanny lack of birdsong and the monotonous desecration of the landscape interrupted only by an occasional timber-lorry.

❖ As the road curves southwards and south-westwards, the route leaves the forest and runs along a valley bottom, forming the rear of the soldier's cloak. Here, the scenery becomes majestic; with breath-taking escarpments and the raw beauty of the mountain-colours of Wales.

❖ Just below Glan-yr-eryr, the road curves westwards and, by the small dwelling of Maes-y-felin, a track to the right is taken; it climbs up the escarpment, completing the form of the human's cloak. Near the top of this track, is a substantial standing stone which, from the valley-bottom, stands out as purposeful and distinctive.

The mountain ridge above, from Esgair Fraith to Garn Fawr was described by Fred Price, author of 'The History of Caio' (1904), as being "bright, sunny, and commanding a very Paradise of the wild and free" and he found it to be an area of numerous cairns and containing the remnants of meaningfully-arranged stones which created the forms of circles and squares, as well as two possible cromlechs. The author went on to explain that the vicinity had been populated, telling that "Along the top of the hill two parallel platforms appear to run; and these are covered with the debris of huts".

Robb relays that the Celtic settlements were often civilised and well-designed; so much so, that, in 52-51 BC, Julius Caesar spent the winter in the Aeduan capital of Bibracte, at a hill-fort settlement of the Celtic Gauls. There, his book 'De Bello Gallico', which included a chapter about the Druids, was scribed.

There was much Caesar respected about the Druids. Robb points out that it was not until around 20 AD that Druidism was first outlawed by the Romans, under the edict of Tiberius and, later, by Claudius around 54 AD. Prior to that, there were occasions of mutual influence and co-operation between the Romans and Celts, as attested by the event of the Druid, Diviciacus, approaching the Roman Senate to request military support, in 63 BC. Robb notes of the Celtic warriors:

"All of them carried brightly painted shields and cloaks fastened at the shoulder with a brooch. Their cloaks and trousers were striped, with checks of many colours. Some of the warriors wore iron-helmets crested with wings or a solar wheel . . . . They might almost have passed as Romans".

❖ Returning to the area of the iron-age helmet of the Sagittarian warrior of the Pumpsaint zodiac; at the southern side of Pont Llanio, a footpath runs westwards to Ystrad-Dewi and then south, south-westwards to a footbridge, where it crosses Afon Teifi.

- ❖ By following the footpath over the river-bridge, the route comes to a fork. Both paths off the fork are pertinent – one leads by an old fort, the other by a bath house.

These routes cover boggy ground, with patches of sorrel growing in abundance. Druids utilised the properties of plants for medicinal and ceremonial purposes and it is notable that "cresses of a purifying quality", as described by Taliesin, can often be found growing near ancient sites; commonly, watercress. Davies believed Taliesin was referring to vervain in his prose; a herb much esteemed by the Druids. Vervain, sorrel and watercress all have purifying properties.

The bath-house and fort are asserted to be Roman. The discovery, on the sites, of the remains of Roman pottery and inscribed Roman stones, dated by Coflein to be from around 73 AD to 130 AD, indicate Roman occupation; but this may not provide conclusive evidence that the architects of the site were Roman.

- ❖ The two tracks re-converge to the west, on the A485.

Significantly, the two paths taken create the outline of an emblem at the fore of the soldier's helmet. It is the image of an oak-leaf; a symbol most sacred to the Druids.

17

Capricorn

Symbol: A hobgoblin

Constellation-symbols alter over time and Petersen describes that the now familiar goat of Capricorn was first portrayed as a 'sea-goat'. The outline selected for this book is of a horned, fish-tailed, goat-like hobgoblin, or Welsh 'pwca'.

The goat has long been a symbol of fertility and is seen as having a capricious quality. The goat-footed god, Pan, was honoured as a procreative nature-god; his rites continue to be celebrated in various ways around the world. In Britain, ancient folk customs such as maypole dancing and hobby-horse festivities, have survived across the centuries; paying tribute, often unconsciously, to masculine potency.

For the ancient people of Britain, who were completely dependent on elemental forces and the land, the production of crops and livestock was essential to survival. Successful fertilization was an act of the beneficent energies of nature; the gods. New life, in all its forms, was sacred.

Carreg-y-Bwci (The Hobgoblin Stone) is situated within the outline of Capricorn, in the area of the sea-goat's head. It resides within an almost circular, embanked enclosure, which may be part of a larger ritual site that has an 'entrance' marked by a standing stone next to the 'Roman' Pumpsaint to Llanio road.

To the west of Carreg-y-Bwci is a stone wall with intermittent single, large upright stones. At right-angles to this wall is a row of mature beech trees which seem to defy the usual growth-stunting effects of such an exposed landscape.

Within the embanked enclosure of Carreg-y-Bwci, itself, there is a small, flat area which has the appearance of being a position from which to look onto the stone and, perhaps, to preside over ceremonies associated with it. The stone is recumbent, but may have once stood erect; equally, it could have lain flat, as an alter-stone.

To the south, south-west of Carreg-y-Bwci, is a much larger, slightly embanked area; big enough to hold a small crowd. On positioning oneself inside this space, it becomes apparent that a hilltop cairn, on Esgair Fraith, is directly behind Carreg-y-Bwci and that there is a likely relationship between the two.

Carreg-y-Bwci is imbued with legends of malevolent happenings should an attempt to move the stone be undertaken, or should one decide to spend the night there. Without a doubt, it is a stone of powerful presence and a site of great significance; the stories attached to it may accurately reflect the level of protection it has received.

❖ From Carreg-y-Bwci, heading briefly northwards along Sarn Helen a right-turn is taken to follow a track running eastwards steeply down the dramatic escarpment to Maes-y-felin. The unmapped, but monumental standing stone near the top of the path has a commanding appearance, one of marking the route to the ceremonial site of Carreg-y-Bwci and calling for attendance.

❖ At Maes-y-felin, a sharp turn to the right along the lane south-westwards is followed for a short stretch, until the road curves to the south. Here, running behind Taldre, a less steeply inclined footpath is taken to 'Bwlch Blaen-corn', which translates as 'pass at the fore of the horn'; suitably so, the route just described arrived at the sea-goat's head and the place from where the horn sprouts.

The tracks just followed are, in themselves, extraordinary; with a nearby easier route up to Carreg-y-Bwci and the top of the mountain-range, via Bwlch Blaen-Corn, the enormous task of carving a track into the almost sheer-sided rock face of the escarpment appears to have been mainly for the purpose of creating the hobgoblin's horn.

❖ Returning to Taldre, a left-turn is taken, continuing along the lane in a southerly direction to Cae-Caradog, after which a fork in the road is reached. By crossing the ford and following the road up to a T-junction, a right-turn leads back up to Bwlch Blaen-corn and the outline of Capricorn's face is shaped. However, by taking the right fork to the ford and then tracking the small river course on the left, the outline of a goat's beard is created.

❖ The back of the hobgoblin's head is defined by turning left at Bwlch Blaen-corn and continuing for a short distance in a westerly direction, before taking a path northwards, skirting along the edge of Pant-teg plantation, but staying with the boundary wall of Pant-teg and the site of Carreg-y-Bwci (passing to the left of the stone), until Sarn Helen is re-joined.

❖ The fore-leg of Capricorn is partially portrayed by following a lane eastwards from Llancrwys (church of the crosses) to Maes-y-fron; turning southwards to Ffarmers and then westwards past Ddol-y-Brenin to a T-junction.

Llancrwys church was initially sited near the standing stone, Carreg hirfaen, within the outline of the hen. The new and current church, now within the effigy of Capricorn, brought the name of 'Llan-y-crwys' with it. Lewis Edwards recorded that the original church was "so named after the Stone of the Three Crosses situated on the boundary between Cardiganshire and Carmarthenshire".

In seeking to understand more about the history of the Stone of the Three Crosses, Edwards learned that there had been a tall menhir in the old churchyard, on which was carved three circles with a small cross in each.

With a 'circle' being a symbol of the old belief system and a 'cross' being a symbol of the new; and with the number 'three' having sacred meaning for them both, this stone might have marked an unspoken declaration of intent; one of peaceful co-existence, of unity and mutual respect. Edwards aptly concluded, "it is worthy of the greatest care".

Although the church was eventually separated from its stones when it moved to its new site, Carreg hirfaen remained in its original position. However, the Stone of the Three Crosses' was uprooted and is reputed to have ended up at Golden Grove, near Llandeilo. This was an insensitive decision and, with each stone in the temple having been selected and placed with care, it is one that the Druids would have been unlikely to make. It is said that the stone emanated a feeling of unrest after its displacement; Edwards reported that "the workmen who moved it to its resting place were disturbed by its characteristics. They said it was an echo stone".

❖ To form the front of the hobgoblin and the top of its partial rear leg; from Llancrwys, a south and then westwards route through Ffaldybrenin is taken, to the first left turn into a lane, which is followed as it runs south, south-eastwards to join the A482.

❖ Following a footpath from Ffaldybrenin south, south-eastwards a place marked on old maps as 'Llwyn wormwood' (which translates as 'wormwood grove') is reached; perhaps referring to a ceremonial use of wormwood in the rites associated with this effigy.

❖ Following the A482, westwards, past Derlwyn and continuing to a crossroad, a right-turn to a junction near Pen-y-bryn is reached. Here, taking the lane on the right, heading in a general north-eastwards direction all the way back to Bwlch-Blaen-corn, the humped-back of the pwca is outlined.

❖ However, taking a left-turn at the junction near Pen-y-bryn a fascinating route is followed, where two large standing stones and one smaller one, mark out the ancient way to a fork in the road. Taking a right-turn here, past Esgair-wen and then a sharp left-turn just to the west of Blaen-Hathren, the way continues until a junction is reached. Here a sharp turn on the left is taken; it runs past Bryn Melyn and returns back to the lane with three standing stones, completing the outline of the sea-goat's fishtail.

Coflein, the online database of the 'National Monuments Record of Wales' (NMRW), describes that Carreg-y-Bwci was initially thought to be a prehistoric monument but, more recently, as a 'Roman tower emplacement'. Certainly, there is much evidence of Roman activity in the area, but it was not unusual for the Romans to make use of already existing Celtic sites. That the Romans should establish themselves within, and around, the Pumpsaint temple is not surprising; they would have been keen to exploit the rich mineral deposits in the locality, of gold, silver and lead.

Inevitably, the Roman presence would have shaped the way in which the Druids conducted their practices. Davies described this process, saying that "The Roman laws and edicts, had for some ages, restrained the more cruel customs, and the bloody sacrifices of the Druids: what now remained was their code of mystical doctrines, together with their symbolic rites."

With many tracks leading to the sign of Capricorn, including the steep path climbing up to Carreg-y-Bwci from the valley below, accompanied by a prominent, towering stone at the top of it, the 'pwca' appears to have held important ritual meaning.

The sheer drama of the 3 levels of terrain, from valley floor rising sharply to Carreg-y-Bwci and, again, steeply upwards to the hilltop cairn on Esgair Fraith are suggestive of the Celtic 'under', 'middle' and 'other' worlds.

It is proposed that while the site of Carreg-y-Bwci may have been utilized by the Romans, it is probable that it is of Celtic origin. This effigy portrays not just the fish-tail goat of Capricorn; but the wider characteristics offer a multi-layered depiction of meaning and belief belonging to the Druid tradition.

18

Concluding thoughts

"The temples and other sacred enclosures that were once a prominent feature of the landscape were constructed as though the heavenly ellipse surrounded them."

Graham Robb, 'The Ancient Paths', 2013.

The sculpting of the constellation-symbols, along with images of the arkite legend, on the landscape around the Dolaucothi gold-mines is a piece of sacred temple-architecture of likely iron-age, Druid origin. Davies' translations of early bardic prose demonstrate that it would have been used for ceremonies and rituals, including the rite of initiation into the Druid mysteries.

The Druids were a people who related to the stars and sky, the land, and the powers and presences of the natural world, with reverence; they were a people who understood the value of symbolism and the art of ritual; their teachings and practices had drawn poets and princes alike.

The Welsh bards described how, in the 6th century AD, there were deliberate assaults on temple sites. However, Davies evidenced that, despite attempts to clear away the old religion, initiations into the Druid mysteries continued until the mid 12th century, at least. It is probable, therefore, that the celestial sanctuaries in Wales, and perhaps this one, continued to be in use for some considerable time.

The placement of this temple would not have been accidental. Graham Robb, in 'The Ancient Paths' explains that the iron-age Celts constructed their roads and sacred sites along uniform lines, connecting one to another by dint of shared mathematical angles which, themselves, held value within their belief system. For example, the angle of the rising summer-solstice sun, or the north-to-south direction of longitudinal lines, might be used to determine where their holy centres should be established, where battles should be fought; or the direction a road should take.

Robb lays out some of the key grid-lines across Gaul and Britain. One such line runs through a place named Medionemeton, in Scotland; a nemeton is a Druidic sacred grove or sanctuary. Following the longitudinal line from Medionemeton, southwards, it continues through the hill-forts of Dinas Emrys, Dinas Oleu, Aberystwyth's Pendinas and onwards to the 'Pumpsaint Temple of the Stars'.

This book has focussed on the area of the temple which contains the constellations of the zodiac. Further images relating to the arkite story have been identified and it could take a few more years of research to attain a fuller picture. For example, Henning tells that the Pendragon Society found an image of a falcon, in the area of Falcondale, on the north, north-east edge of Lampeter. He describes that a standing stone, with a paternoster cross cut into it, is now built into the walls of Falcondale Lodge. The stone's original position is unknown, but it is believed that it previously stood nearby.

It is of particular interest that the proposed falcon outline lies beneath 'Temple Bar'. In 'A Guide to Glastonbury's Temple of the Stars', Maltwood explained told that, in the 14th century legend, King Arthur rode into Castle Cary and saw "at the entrance a spear set bar-wise (horizontally), and looketh to the right". If, in times gone by, the setting of a spear at an entrance was a commonplace method of conveying a message, then it gives rise to the possibility that 'Temple Bar' was the location of an entrance to the Pumpsaint sanctuary, perhaps one with an administrative function.

Lewis Edwards proposed that the main entrance to the temple was in Pisces and Graham Robb found that the gateway to Druidic sites usually lay in the north-east; in this temple, the position of the mystical gryphon.

Intriguingly, about five miles to the north-east of the Pumpsaint Temple, is a relatively short, but steep, route across the mountains named 'Cwrs yr Ychain-banog'. It lies to the east of the swampy ground of Afon Teifi and translates as 'course of the sacred bulls'. There are cairns at the eastern end of it.

It is unclear whether 'Cwrs yr Ychain-banog' was once believed to be the site of the origins of the story of the deluge in Wales, or if it was a processional track used for later ceremonial purposes. Davies told that Welsh legend conveyed something had happened to one of the sacred bulls, recording that "One of these oxen overstrained himself, in drawing forth the 'avanc', so that his eyes started from their sockets, and he dropped down dead, as soon as the feat was achieved." He went on to record that one of the surviving oxen "wandered about disconsolate", at the loss of his companion, until he died at *"Brevi"*, meaning *"bellowing"*.

That the arkite myth was etched onto the earth at all; that its story was solemnly re-enacted by the early Celts and preserved by the Welsh bards in their prose; that, as late as the early 19th century, the partial re-telling of it was "still vigorous in every corner of the principality", might seem remarkable. However, the effort and dedication involved in the construction of the temple reveals something of the mindset of the architects.

Pertinently, the Druids were an educated, skilled and imaginative community who were orientated to the gods of the natural world and deeply thankful for their provision. They were also invested in the continuity and preservation of their legends, which incorporated hidden sacred meanings.

Moreover, with their observations that wondrous celestial-beings were closely connected to the seasonal cycle of the year, along with a belief in the re-birth of the human soul, the Druids were led to build by stone and by star; for endurance and for eternity.

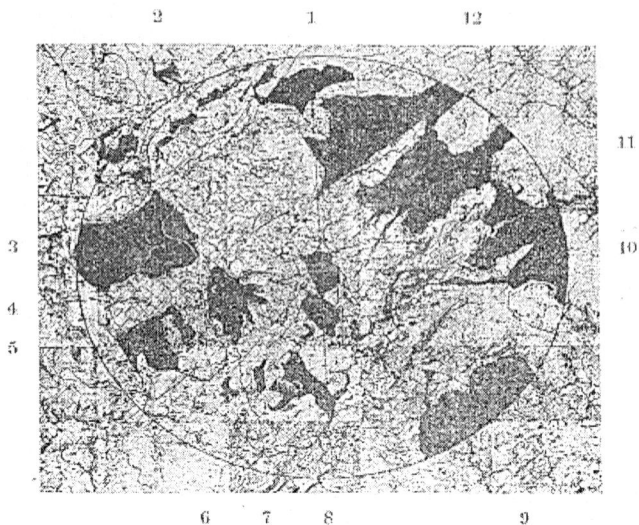

1. Aquarius (Squirrel).
2. Pisces (Two Fishes).
3. Aries (Ram).
4. Taurus (Bull's Head).
5. Orion (Man's Head & Arm).
6. Argo Navis (Boat).
7. Unindentified.

8. Leo (Lion).
9. Virgo (Sheaf & Body).
10. Scorpio (Scorpion & Eagle).
11. Sagittarius (Man on Horse with Lance).
12. Capricorn (Unicorn).

Lewis Edwards' Map of the Temple of the Stars 1947

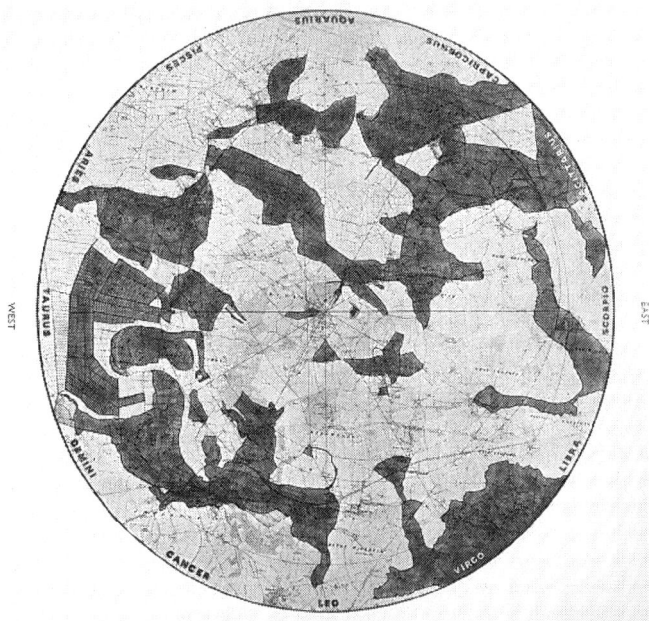

Glastonbury Map of the Temple of the Stars:
K Maltwood, 1937

Bibliography
References

Books and articles referred to:

Allcroft: Hadrian, A (1927); 'Circle and The Cross: A Study in Continuity, The Circle Part 1'. London: MacMillan and Co. Limited. Re-printed Breinigsville, PA, USA: Kessinger Publishing's Rare Reprints (2010).

Chris Barber and John Godfrey Williams (1989); 'The Ancient Stones of Wales'. Abergavenny: Blorenge Books.

Chronicles 1:10; 'Holy Bible' (1930). London: British and Foreign Bible Society.

Davies, E, (1809); 'The Mythology and Rites of the British Druids'. London: J Booth. Re-printed Memphis USA: General Books LLC, 2012.

Edwards, Lewis (1948); 'The Welsh Temple of the Zodiac'. Atlantean Research, Vol 1 (1948) nos. 2,3,4.

Ezekiel 10; 'Holy Bible' (1930). London: British and Foreign Bible Society.

Frazer, Sir James George (1949); The Golden Bough, 'A Study in Magic and Religion'. London: MacMillan and Co Ltd.

Koch, John T. (2006); *Celtic Culture: A Historical Encyclopaedia' (5 volumes)*. Santa Barbara and Oxford: ABC-CLIO Ltd.

Maltwood, K.E (1934); 'A Guide to Glastonbury's Temple of the Stars'. London: John Watkins. Re-printed Victoria BC, Canada: Victoria Printing and Publishing Co., 1950.

Maltwood, K.E (1937); 'Air View Supplement to A Guide to Glastonbury's Temple of the Stars'. London: John, M, Watkins.

Packenham, Thomas (2001); 'Meetings with Remarkable Trees'. London: Cassell & Co.

Parker, J and Parker, D (1991); 'Parker's Astrology'. London: Dorling Kindersley Ltd.

Robb, G (2013); 'The Ancient Paths'. Basingstoke and Oxford: Picador, an imprint of Pan Macmillan.

Online sources:

http://www.britishlistedbuildings.co.uk/wa-10906-church-of-st-michael-cilycwm#.WLQJHrdvjctW D Caroe. Anglican parish church, C14 and C15, restored 1905-9

http://www.britishmuseum.org/research/collection_online/collection_object_details.aspx?objectId=368264&partId=1

https://www.ceredigion.gov.uk/utilities/action/act_download.cfm?mediaid=13555&langtoken=cym

http://cilycwm.com/historygroup/?page_id=345

http://*www.coflein.gov.uk/en/site/303905/details/carreg-y-bwci*

Peter Cornah (Nov. 2001); http://www.cilycwm.com/?page_id=76

http://www.cothichurches.org.uk/Llanfihangel/History/Early_history_of_llanfihangel.htmTaken from notes by Canon Patrick Thomas. A Lost Church and a Hammer-Throw

http://www.llanddewibrefi.org/history/*Based on extracts from 'Yr Ancr' magazine, research work completed by pupils of Ysgol Gynradd Llanddewi Brefi in the 1970's and their Headmaster, the late Mr. Ben Richards.*

https://mesocosm.net/2011/12/22/the-tetramorph-the-sumerian-origins-of-a-christian-symbol/

Morien Institute;
http://www.morien-institute.org/pumpsaint.html

National Trust; http://www.nationaltrust.org.uk/dolaucothi-gold-mines

J.K. Petersen (2016); http://voynichportal.com/tag/zodiac-signs/

Price; F S. (1904); History of Caio, Carmarthenshire. Reproduced by http: //books.google.com/

Ridpath, I; http://www.ianridpath.com/startales/orion2.htm

Schwabe, C, W (1978); 'Cattle, Priests and Medicine', Vol.4, at p. 16 (U. of Minn. 1978), cited on wikipaedia; http://en.wikipedia.org/wiki/nose_ring_(animal)

Freddy Silva; http://www.invisibletemple.com/stone-in-sacred-sites.html

The Guardian, (2017); http://www.theguardian.com/artanddesign/2017/jan/19/fourth-plinth-shortlist-trafalgar-square-winged-bull

Jeffrey L. Thomas (2009); http://www.castlewales.com/talley.html

Thompson Gary D; The Origin of the Zodiac Copyright (© 2001-2016); http://members.westnet.com.au/gary-davidthompson/page9a.html

John Vinycomb, [1909]; *Fictitious and Symbolic Creatures in Art*, by, at sacred-texts.com; http://www.sacred texts.com/lcr/fsca/fsca34.htm

Wikipedia; https://en.wikipedia.org/wiki/Talley_Abbey

John Wiles, RCAHMW, 26 February (2008); http://map.coflein.gov.uk/index.php?action=do_details&numlink=303530

Made in the USA
Columbia, SC
22 November 2017